Jörn W. Scheer (Ed
Crossing Borders – Going

CW01022991

The Psychology of Personal Constructs, developed by George A. Kelly (1905-1967), stressed the importance of the meanings that individuals attach to persons and events in the world surrounding them. Consequently it has been branded as an 'individualistic' theory neglecting the social nature of the *Human Condition*. However, in a Personal Construct Psychology view, the notion of *The Other* includes members of a wider community, of cultural groups, and even members of other nations. In this book, scholars from several countries write about issues of cross-cultural relevance, such as international travel, the importance of language, the unification and dissolution of states, migration to a new country, and what all this means for the definition, maintenance and development of the individual's identity.

Some of the papers have been published before but are out of print or difficult to access. Included is Kelly's famous paper on 'Europe's Matrix of Decision' that has not been available for a number of years.

Jörn W. Scheer (Ed.)

Crossing Borders –
Going Places

Personal Constructions
of Otherness

Psychosozial-Verlag

Editor:
Prof. Dr. phil. Dipl.-Psych. Jörn W. Scheer
Abteilung für Medizinische Psychologie
Zentrum für Psychosomatische Medizin
Justus-Liebig-Universität Giessen
Friedrichstr. 36
35392 Giessen
Germany

Bibliografische Information Der Deutschen Bibliothek
Die Deutsche Bibliothek verzeichnet diese Publikation in der Deutschen
Nationalbibliografie; detaillierte bibliografische Daten sind im Internet
über <http://dnb.ddb.de> abrufbar.

© 2003 Psychosozial-Verlag / Haland & Wirth
Goethestr. 29, D-35390 Gießen
Tel.: 0641/77819; Fax: 0641/77742
www.psychosozial-verlag.de
Alle Rechte vorbehalten, insbesondere das der Vervielfältigung und
Verbreitung sowie der Übersetzung, Mikroverfilmung, Einspeicherung
und Verarbeitung in elektronischen oder optischen Systemen, der öffentli-
chen Wiedergabe durch Hörfunk-, Fernsehsendungen und Mulitmedia
sowie der Bereithaltung in einer Online-Datenbank oder im Internet zur
Nutzung durch Dritte.
Umschlaggestaltung: Christof Röhl
nach Entwürfen des Ateliers Warminski, Büdingen
Printed in Germany
ISDN 3-89806-296-1

Contents

ON OTHERNESS

Appendix

Contributors

Peter Cummins, Psychological Services, Gulson Hospital, Coventry, UK. *petercummins@dial.pipex.com*

Dorota Dobosz-Bourne, Graduate Business School, University of Luton, Putteridge Bury Management Centre. *dorota.dobosz@luton.ac.uk*

Devi Jankowicz, Prof., Ph. D., Graduate Business School, University of Luton, Putteridge Bury Management Centre. *devi.jankowicz@luton.ac.uk*

George A. Kelly, Deceased

James C. Mancuso, em. Prof., University at Albany, Albany, NY, USA. *mancusoj@capital.net*

Jörn W. Scheer, em. Prof. Dr., Dept. of Medical Psychology, Centre for Psychosomatic Medicine, University of Giessen, Germany. *joern.scheer@joern-scheer.de*

Du_an Stojnov, Prof., Ph.D., Dept. of Psychology, Fakulty of Philosophy, University of Belgrade, Serbia-Montenegro. *dstojnov@f.bg.ac.yu*

Beverly Walker, Ph.D., Prof., Dept. of Psychology, University of Wollongong, N.S.W, Australia. *beverly_walker@uow.edu.au*

Bill Warren, Ph.D., Prof., Faculty of Education, University of Newcastle, NSW, Australia. *edwgw@cc.newcastle.edu.au*

Introduction

When *George Alexander Kelly* (1905–1967) published 'The Psychology of Personal Constructs' in 1955, it was heralded by some as a breakthrough in modern psychology. Since then, however, PCP (as it is commonly abbreviated) has been pigeon-holed in mainstream psychology as one of several 'cognitive personality theories' of merely historical importance. In clinical psychology, Kelly's own realm, the PCP approach has at best been allocated a niche in the vicinity of other 'humanistic' schools. Whereas quite a few researchers and practitioners have adopted Kelly's contribution to the methods of assessment, the 'Repertory Grid Technique', they have often done so without reference to its theoretical context. And even the 'constructivist turn' of late rarely acknowledges the revolutionary potential of Kelly's theory. On the contrary, social constructionists tend to dismiss Kelly's approach as inappropriately individualistic. In fact, Kelly's insistence on the relevance of the individual's view (in other words, the *personal* construing of events and people) has often obscured that this approach implies the general importance of (and respect for) The Other: not only the client or a family member or other 'relevant others', but also members of a wider community, including cultural groups, and even members of other nations.

Kelly himself has laid the ground for applying personal construct theory to cross-cultural matters when he travelled to a number of countries and interviewed people about their views of crucial issues they and their countries were facing. 'Europe's matrix of decision', published in 1962, was the result of this endeavour. It took a while before PCP scholars followed him in that direction. 'The construction of group realities' (1996, edited by Kalekin-Fishman and Walker) was the first systematic attempt to explore culturally determined constructions from a PCP perspective. Now, more than a generation later, a changed world characterised by global politics, multinational economics, mass communication and intercontinental travel has put the necessity of an improved cross-cultural understanding irrepressibly on the agenda. If this world is to survive, we must be able to 'construe the constructions' of peoples that are far away from us in a multiple sense, geographically, culturally and emotionally, even if we don't share their constructions. In Kelly's terms, what is called for is *sociality* – beyond experienced *commonality*.

Scholars involved in PCP have responded to this challenge in a variety of ways. PCP itself has become an international movement that has transcended the boundaries of Anglo-American culture. In this volume, a number of essays have been assembled that deal with 'crossing borders' from a personal construct theory perspective. The majority of them have been published before, but they are either out of print or appeared in books that are difficult to access. Some appear for the first time in English, some have been written specially for this volume.

Crossing borders: Kelly's paper, mentioned above, has been reprinted in the 1996 book edited by Kalekin-Fishman and Walker but has been out of print for a number of years. It is presented here again, together with a re-assessment that *Peter Cummins* undertook in 1999. Peter Cummins also analyses what the Channel tunnel, the 'chunnel', in a way the final blow to Britannia's 'Splendid Isolation', means for the relationship between Britain and (the rest of) Europe. And *Jörn Scheer* discusses what happened between the two German states when the iron-and-concrete borders that had separated them for almost half a century suddenly disappeared.

Going places: In a way, our civilisation can be considered a culture of travellers. We travel for holiday and leisure, for business and information, both literally and metaphorically crossing borders all the time, and we have to re-construe, i.e. revise our constructions permanently, as *Beverly Walker* shows in her essays on travelling from a constructivist point of view. *Jörn Scheer* utilises the Repertory Grid Technique to analyse how a well-known tourist destination, the German capital city of Berlin, is construed by a group of professional travellers: participants of an international PCP congress.

Speaking in tongues: When fifty days after the Crucifixion a group of believers 'spoke in tongues' they were able to use languages they had never learned to proclaim the gospel to natives of far-away countries. On the other hand, the Babel experience points to the difficulties posed by the existence of so many different languages. *Jörn Scheer* addresses the problems arising when one language has emerged as the dominant one in world culture while *Devi Jankowicz* and *Dorota Dobosz*, both bilingual, show how simply translating terms is not sufficient to transport meanings from one language group to another. A process of negotiation is required to 'let ideas travel'.

On Otherness: The final section deals with core issues of our *Human Condition*, that is, our identity. Our identity is to a large extent determined by how we construe ourselves as members of cultural and national groups – and 'different from others'. *Peter Cummins*, an Irishman in England, and *James Mancuso*, an American descendant of Italian migrants, discuss the importance of the 'located self' and the interactions between 'new' and 'old' migrants – after all, most members of 'established culture groups' everywhere in the world are descendants of migrants themselves – the Anglo-Saxons in the United States as well as the Aborigines in Australia. This is also at the core of *Bill Warren*'s essay on the personal construction of the social-cultural context in which modern day Australians find themselves in relation to their land's indigenous peoples. When *Du_an Stojnov* discusses the tragic consequences of antagonistic ways of construing handed down over generations in the peoples of former Yugoslavia, we may see that the Theory of Personal Constructs can not only serve as a useful tool in the professional context, as in clinical psychology, management or education, but also has the potential to inspire and inform the endeavour to increase the understanding for other ways of construing than our own.

We may then be able to see *otherness* not as a threat but as an invitation.

In keeping with the focus of the theory on personal constructions, the papers presented here have a 'personal' touch also in a different sense. The authors don't hide behind the language and posture of scientific research. Because I invited most of these papers at different occasions, some of the authors found it appropriate to acknowledge this fact in an overly flattering way. Although good manners would have required eliminating these passages I left the papers unchanged, to preserve the personal nature of the texts as they were written originally. I feel privileged to be able to present these authors' views, their experiences and their constructions.

I also thank the University of Nebraska Press for the permission to reprint Kelly's paper that started it all, and the Australian Psychological Society for the permission to reprint one of my own efforts.

Jörn Scheer

Hamburg (Germany), July 2003

CROSSING BORDERS

Europe's Matrix of Decision[1]

*George A. Kelly**

There is something you all should know at the outset of this paper: I have no use for the concept of motivation. Professor Jones was well aware of this last summer when he invited me to come here. We were having coffee together in Copenhagen—at least I remember it as coffee, although Dr. Jones says it was tea. I believe our wives were with us at the time. He doesn't remember that either. At any rate, he remembers that he invited me to come here. At the time, we both found the idea of my having to talk in public about motivation highly amusing. He probably still thinks it is funny, but, after the toil of preparing this paper, I am not so sure I still do. Nevertheless, here I am.

Since that conversation I have pondered on a number of things, including the whimsical possibility of writing such a convincing paper that you would be moved to change the topic of this annual Nebraska conclave to "Snakes in Ireland." How much more to the point it would be if the topic were something like this: "What Is Everybody up to These Days?" or "What in the World Is Mankind about To Do to Itself?" or perhaps this one: "Isn't There Any Other Way of Coping with a Problem Besides Lying Down and Being Treated for It?" A good short title could, I think, be lifted from Hans Fallada's 1932 novel, *Little Man, What Now?* "The Nebraska Symposium on *What Now"* — not bad!

Let us be honest with ourselves—isn't this the persistent question we hope to answer by all our talk about motivation: How can we forecast human behavior when it is left on its own? Not that this is a particularly well-posed question either, for I am sure you could argue, on the one hand, that human behavior is never on its own, or, on the other, that it is always on its own. Nevertheless, what we are trying to get at are the internal predicates of behavior, as contrasted with those external predicates we can more clearly and comfortably envision, such as stimuli or the inescapable logic we assume to be inherent in the way things are.

I. WHAT IT MEANS TO UNDERSTAND MEN IN TERMS OF THEIR CONSTRUCTS

This paper is essentially a continuation of one I presented in the spring of 1957 as part of the *Syracuse University Symposium on the Assessment of*

---

[1] The experiences upon which this paper is based were made possible by a grant to the writer and his wife from the Human Ecology Fund.

Human Motives. In that paper—which was published, along with the other contributions, under the editorship of Gardner Lindzey, and is now available in a paperback edition (Kelly, 1958)—I stated my theoretical position under the title, "Man's Construction of His Alternatives."

In my present paper I want to talk about the application of the theory to a specific international problem; the European man's construction of his alternatives. In this way I hope, not only to show how the theory works, but also to throw some light on an important substantive problem. You see, I have brazenly gone ahead with my distortion of the topic of this symposium and am speaking as if it were already "The Nebraska Symposium on *What Now.*"

Theoretical Springboard

Before I launch into today's topic, however, I had better sketch some of the more important features of my theoretical position. Motivation is an invented construct. It cropped up a long time ago as a by-product of certain pre-Socratic assumptions about the fundamental nature of things. Once upon a time, there was a division of opinion between the Eleatic School of Parmenides, which assumed that fundamentally objects were solid and inert, and Heraclitus, who wanted to start with the assumption that change was the one inescapable fact of existence. Neither side won the argument outright, but, as far as history is concerned, Heraclitus came out the worse. Atomism, which was a sort of compromise worked out later by Democritus and others, eventually caught hold and, off and on, has pretty much held its own ever since.

The crux of the matter is that if you start with the assumption that whatever the world is made of must be inherently inert, you then have to go ahead and guess that it changes only as force is applied to it. Here you are, saddled with two distinct constructs; objects, and the force that makes them move. As long as you are a materialist—and nearly everybody is, in spite of what he says—there is not much else you can do except think in terms of primary objects, such as the atoms of Democritus, being pushed around by secondary forces.

Apply this basic thinking to physiology, and you have the notion of a body being actuated by energy; apply it to psychology, and you come up with the notion of a person either being propelled by "motives" in spite of himself, or stuck tight in his fundament. As I say, there is just not much else you can do about it, unless you are willing to go back to about 420 B.C. and start thinking all over.

Well, I suggested in the Syracuse Symposium that we should go back and start over. Suppose we began by assuming that the fundamental thing about life is that it goes on. It isn't that something *makes* it go on; the going on *is the thing itself.* It isn't that motives *make* man come alert and do things; his alertness is an aspect of his very being. Talking about activating motives is simply redundant talky-talk, for once you've got a human being on your hands, you already have alertness and movement, and sometimes a lot more of it than you know what to make of.

There is another habit of thinking that Western Man more or less fell into fortuitously. As long as he was assuming that human beings are propelled by motives, it seemed reasonable to imagine also that the motives give direction to the movement; if they push, they must push in some direction. Now if we could only find out what is pushing, we could predict where everybody is going, as well as how soon he would get there.

So for two thousand years we have been looking for the thing that is doing the pushing, and often trying to define it by the directions it pushes. We haven't found it yet; naturally we haven't found it, but during the centuries we have built up a tremendous lexicon of push and pull terms. Even our language has fallen heir to the design of our quest, and we have committed ourselves to a grammar of motives (Burke, 1945) that controls our speech and channels our thinking about human behavior. Now we can scarcely say anything about what a person has done, or is about to do, without using a language form that implies that he has been pushed into it. We are even inclined to think that way about our own behavior, and when we do, it usually means we are in trouble.

But there is another way of accounting for the direction man's behavior takes, besides assuming that it must be imparted by the same forces that make him behave in the first place. We can start by saying that man copes with his environment by construing it into similarities and contrasts. It is not necessary to assume that this is a verbal or conscious undertaking. The associations and distinctions can be made at a very low level of awareness, as psychological research on reflexes has amply demonstrated.

The Personal Construct

The unit form of this construing can be designated as the *construct,* an abstraction of the linkage and differentiation which, inside each man's own tight little world, constitutes a generalized pair of alternatives. The construct, being an abstraction, can be picked up, carried around, and fitted to a great variety of circumstances. If it has a verbal handle on it, so much the better; it is easier to transport. A system of constructs constitutes a ready-made format for future thinking, and for lower order processes as well. To have constructed such a system means that a person has somewhat prepared himself to cope with all sorts of strange things that have not happened yet. But without it he is not free to think, to act, or even to get the gist of what is going on.

14

When a person can apply a construct to his own behavior, consciously or unconsciously, it opens for him a channel of choice along which he is more or less free to move. But without such a channel his freedom has no dimension, no extent; he cannot even strive toward objectives, nor can he hope for things to come, nor long for something out of reach, for he has no idea of what he is missing, nor even any sense of missing at all. He can no more move about in lines he has not construed than he can use the fourth dimension to side-step a locked door. This is why, throughout the history of the world, men seeking what they supposed to be freedom have struggled heroically to change their masters, but have made only feeble efforts to loosen their chains.

Get some notion of what a person's system of channels is like and you have a rough sketch of the network within which he is prepared to exercise his human right to freedom. Observe the shrinkage of a man s system, and you find yourself a witness to a gradual human enslavement, enslavement without barbed wire or coercion. It is this enslavement by atrophy of ideas that we sometimes call institutionalized behavior. We are usually thinking about mental hospitals, prisons, and orphans' asylums when we use the term, but the same kind of enslavement can occur in societies and in nations. Understanding a man's construct system is, then, the first, and most important, step in understanding what is commonly known by that vaguest of psychological terms, "motivation." And it is also the first step in comprehending the actual extent of a man's freedom. I was talking about this final step when I presented my Syracuse paper on ''Man's Construction of His Alternatives.''

Having construed his alternatives, a man still has to make choices between them if he is to commit himself to any undertaking. As a matter of fact, there are two kinds of choices he must make; the selection from his repertory of the most relevant construct to apply to his circumstances, and his choice between the pair of alternatives which that construct presents. There are some psychological principles that govern these choices, but there is no need to expound them here.

This concludes the review of what I said at Syracuse University. It was a theoretical statement, and it was my effort to extricate our thinking from the underlying assumptions upon which the notion of motivation is based, as well as from the deeply ingrained notion of motivation itself.

A Method of Studying Attitudes

This kind of theorizing leads us next, as all good theorizing should, to a methodology, and from methodology to substance, all the while being subject to successive revisions in the light of its outcomes. There are many ramifications of the methodology I am about to describe; ramifications in psychotherapy, in teaching, in negotiation, and in psychometrics. But let me confine myself to one area only; the theory's methodological implications in the appraisal of attitudes having international implications.

It is customary, in studying attitudes, to focus upon certain parameters. We may examine the object or the class of objects embraced by the attitude. We may take account of the attitude's generality across a wide variety of objects. We may judge its consonance with the rest of the attitudinal system and its stability from moment to moment. We may estimate its tendency to express itself in overt action. We may attempt to measure its intensity by estimating the amount of effort that is likely to be mobilized in its behalf. We may note its rigidity in the face of negating experience; and we may appraise its rational status, or look to see how deeply it is rooted in unconscious processes.

All these approaches are similar in one respect; they assume that an attitude is a one-sided affair—a man likes blondes or he does not. The attitude presumably has to do with blondes, and blondes only, which, I am sure some of you will agree, is a pretty one-sided way of looking at things. What in the world does it mean, merely to say that a man likes blondes? Does it mean he likes them rather than hates them, that he likes them better than brunettes, or does it mean he likes them better than doing his own cooking? We suppose there is some dimension along which differentiation is being made, but unless we look for the direction in which the opposite pole lies, we cannot tell what the bewildered fellow has on his mind.

A man says he despises capitalism. Does this mean he is a communist? Or does it mean he favors an economic democracy analogous to the political democracy that was achieved in Western Europe after centuries of struggle and bloodshed? Or can we stretch his statement to mean, on the contrary, that he opposes all forms of government by consent of the governed?

We don't really know what the statement means to the man who made it until we know the issue at stake. One of us might say that, in order to make such a remark, he would have to be a totalitarian of some sort—either a communist or a fascist—because it seems so downright certain that those are the only logical alternatives to capitalism. At least, the fellow must be against human dignity, because we are convinced the capitalism he despises is the natural expression of any society where personal liberties are respected. We may be rights of course—perfectly right; but let us keep in mind that these are the similarities and contrasts of our personal construct system, not necessarily of his. It is by such channels that our flow of thought is facilitated and constrained. But his intellectual efforts may be just as inescapably guided by the ruts worn deep in his way of life, even though they may seem utterly irrational to us.

Personal construct theory approaches attitudes by examining issues. It finds

16

these issues, not so much in man's circumstances, as in his way of making sense out of what surrounds him. Purposeful behavior is a matter of setting up alternatives among his surroundings and, when the time comes, choosing between them. This is not an altogether novel approach; Mark Twain, in a behavioristic description of an elephant written long before John B. Watson's time, once made use of it (Clemens, 1896).[2]

Seeking Access to an Alien Dimension of Life

How can we use this approach of personal construct theory, in place of the motivational approach, to understand our friend who says he despises capitalism? Before we make the attempt, it is only fair to warn you that it is always hazardous to look at things through another person's glasses, whether he is a Russian, an Eichmann, a Negro, a psychotic patient, or one's own child—perhaps most of all, one's own child. Looking through glasses that are not your own can permanently affect your eyesight. It is much safer to attribute the behavior of other people to their Motivation—much safer Now, you 'ye been warned!

Let us suppose this man we are talking about is a Georgian, a citizen of that ancient little country, now one of the Soviet Republics, that lies just south of the main ridge of the Caucasus Mountains. When he talks about capitalism he undoubtedly has a vivid picture in mind of the privately controlled economic power of pre-revolutionary Georgian landowners—called princes—who held that it was a waste of time and money to teach farmers to read and write.

There is a painting in the world-famed Hermitage Museum in Leningrad that gives poignant meaning to this Georgian's thoughts about capitalism. It depicts a boy in ragged clothes listening furtively at the crack of a school room door. This picture has deep and far-reaching significance to the people of Eastern Europe. It would probably mean something quite different to an American who imagines the only normal response of boy to school is to play hooky.

The picture is not only symbolic; it is accurately representative. I talked to a man who, as a child, had done just that in his native country of Georgia. But he was soon caught in his delinquency, and the door was slammed in his face.

---

[2] "He will leave Bibles to eat bricks, he will leave bricks to eat bottles, he will leave bottles to eat clothing, he will leave clothing to eat cats, he will leave cats to eat oysters, he will leave oysters to eat ham, he will leave ham to eat sugar, he will leave sugar to eat pie, he will leave pie to eat potatoes, he will leave potatoes to eat bran, he will leave bran, to eat hay, he will leave hay to eat oats, he will leave oats to eat rice, for he was mainly raised on it. There is nothing whatever that he will not eat but European butter, and he would eat that if he could taste it."

Some time after, his father, touched by the boy's disappointment, managed to save back a sack of grain from the family's meager food supplies, and, taking his boy by the hand, carried the grain to the house of the prince. He told the prince the sack of grain was all he had and he asked if, in return for it, his son could be taught to read and write. The prince called the boy to his desk, showed him how to write his name, and then said, "There, young man; that is all the reading and writing you will ever need to know.

The prince kept the grain, possibly as an object lesson in sound economics. Indeed, one must admit that not many people would consider education a proper form of *capital* investment, particularly for one's last sack of grain. This is not to overlook the fact that there are always some people, even in our own country, who will yell for unrealistic expenditures on education—right up to the last Cadillac.

There was, until a few years ago, a somewhat less defensible practice which land-owners in that part of the world were able to enforce by means of their private control of the capital resources of the agricultural community. Brides were required to sleep with the land-owner before they could be claimed by their husbands. This was not quite as bad as it sounds. There was a way out for the groom, if he happened to be an enterprising young man. He was always perfectly free to give up his farm and look for another landlord—one whom he would be more willing to have sleep with his bride, or one who could be bought off for a price within his means. If he were a really imaginative young fellow he could look for a bride with whom nobody would want to sleep; then he could keep his home, his farm, and have a chaste wife besides.

I don't want to leave the wrong impression about Georgia either; this sort of practice was discontinued after the communist revolution and the advent of a man greatly admired in those parts, a fellow by the name of Joseph Stalin. Moreover, none of this has much to do with American capitalism, for it is obviously not the sort of practice that many American landlords could enforce and survive long enough to brag about it. I am only describing the system of capitalistic free enterprise my Georgian friend has in mind when he says he "despises capitalism." Moreover, I suspect this glimpse of the world through his glasses helps us understand what makes him tick better than would any concept of motivation. But as I warned you before, such surreptitious peeks are likely to affect our own eyesight; so it might be just as well if you forgot what I have just told you.

My other friend, the one who wanted to learn to read and write, also made out pretty well in the end, which goes to show what initiative and gumption will do. He took advantage of the confusion of World War I to escape to America. He is now an author and sculptor, and his writings are full of warmth, humor, and love of this country, with none of the bitterness one might expect (Papashvily & Papashvily, 1945, 1946a, 1946b). He is also a great hero back in Georgia, where we shared some experiences together during a recent visit. His American-born wife, in speaking the next morning of one reception they were given the day before, said it was the first time she had been kissed by a whole town.

A Prelude to Action

The other young men of Georgia also took matters in their own hands. My wife and I visited one of their schools a few months ago, along with the friends I have been talking about. We saw the emphasis upon the fundamentals of education—mathematics, languages, science, etc., just as you have heard it reported. One of the men teachers, overwhelmed at meeting the famous Georgian-American author, whose books he had read, embraced him and said, "You are the only person who ever made me cry.

The next day we visited one of the Pioneer Palaces and saw something of the program that provides for the hours, the days, and the months when young people are not in school. Here, in a program as extensive, as competently staffed, and more lavishly equipped than that of the schools, we saw what would be called "frills" in American education. Some observers have come back from the Soviet Union dismissing the Pioneer program as "something like the Boy Scouts." The comparison is preposterous, and the inference, so frequently made, that Soviet education is confined to good old fundamentals, is completely out of line with the facts.

I am still trying to illustrate the application of personal construct theory, in contrast to motivational theory, to the understanding of human behavior. I am trying to sketch a personal dimension of thought which, simply because it is personal and bears on immediate circumstances, represents so clearly the channel of choice for millions of people in Eastern Europe. The channel has to do with education and, strange as it may seem, I think you will agree it also has to do with the dignity of man, or perhaps you will at least agree that it has to do with the dignity of brides. I am inviting you to examine this principal construct dimension, not from our own point of view or as if it were the channel of choice which must govern our own actions, but from the point of view of those whose behavior we hope to understand.

Look at it. On the one end is the private control of capital and on the other, communism—the first step toward which is regarded as state capitalism, the present stage of the Soviet society. I am sure the line between these poles will remain the visible channel of choice until the people of that country are able to conceptualize their circumstances along other dimensions.

Can we "motivate" these people to go in other directions? I think not. Put pressure on them, put them under extreme conditions of need, jam their families into one-room apartments, deny them Cadillacs, ZILs or Volgas, even take away their spare sacks of grain to support the schools, and you will not shoo them like a flock of chickens into our form of society. They will only sigh and say, "Times are hard, food is scarce, and something may be rotten in the administration. Still misfortune has not completely overtaken us; our children are being educated and our wives are respected. Perhaps we will have to go back to the days of 'capitalism'—but it hasn't happened yet. And anyone who wants to drive us back had better remember Stalingrad!" (Or would they say "Volgograd" now?)

Nothing that I have said should be taken to mean that the Soviet empire is ideologically monolithic. To be sure, one finds a remarkable internalization of the ideological controls, to use Don Marquis' phrase for it. People actually do think in the grooves marked out for them, certainly to a much larger extent than do the people of Czechoslovakia, where there are memories of a different kind of society. There are, again, some other dimensions of Georgian thought which permit a vision of the future not approved by Moscow. Nevertheless, whatever those other dimensions are, the one channel I have described is crystal clear to Georgians and is a key to their behavior.

The Construct as a Daily Way of Life

In delineating this Georgian construct I have dwelt mostly on community behavior, that is to say, the forms of behavior that are either articulated outright by group consensus or simply perpetuated by tacit compliance. But what does the construct mean at the level of everyday "spontaneous" behavior—if I may use a familiar, but relatively meaningless, motivational term. Or, to put it this way, which is better, does this construct' have anything to say about what people do when they haven't bothered to go through any complicated process of making up their minds to it? If it does not have anything to do with such everyday individual matters, then our reading of this dimension of Soviet life is probably academic and does not meet the validity criteria that personal construct theory requires. Let us see.

Before entering the Soviet Union my wife and I were more or less aware, as I suppose most Americans are, of the Union's vigorous efforts to put education on a broad popular base, one that is even broader than our own, and not only to permit, but to insure the advanced education of every capable student, regardless of his age, his financial resources, or his formal educational credentials. We knew that some observers have questioned the breadth of this popular base—apart from the fact that the Soviets do not as yet have the total resources comparable to those America has mobilized for the support of education—and we pressed to find out what the restrictions might be. Our observations were mixed and inconclusive on this point, but that the base is very broad, there can be little doubt.[3] I need not go into the detailed ramifica-

---

[3] The American Embassy in Moscow interprets the recent policy changes requiring applicants for university admission to have had two years of work experience—except in fields such as science and engineering technology where personnel shortages exist, or in cases of unusual scholarship—to mean that ideological tests are to be used more ruthlessly in screening students. The student strike at the University of Leningrad in support of the Hungarian uprising, caused Moscow no little concern. Still, outside of the disappearance of the leaders of the strike, presumably to spend the rest of their lives raising corn in areas of Asia where rainfall is at a minimum, and trying to remedy the chaotic condition of Soviet agriculture, no conspicuous measures were taken to enforce ideological conformity among students. There may have been, however, more gradual and subtle measures taken that I do not know about.

Regarding restriction of the popular base of higher education, other reports suggest a quiet but systematic elimination of Jewish students from the universities. We ourselves saw nothing that would confirm these reports, and such information as we were able to infer suggested that the main restrictions might be on somewhat different grounds. For example, the promise of occupational productivity within the socialistic system, particularly in skills believed to be underdeveloped, did seem to be extensively used in selecting students. This selection restriction roughly corresponds to our own preferential support for athletes who show promise of making sports page headlines, and for engineering students who have committed their services to large industrial organizations. It was amusing to see how some students circumvent these preferential restrictions, just as they do in this country.

There is nothing that quite seems to parallel our recent large-scale movement toward restricting higher education to students of more than average means, through the sharp increases of student fees in state-supported universities—measures which are intentionally undertaken—and through our growing imbalance of financial resources between the lower third and the upper two-thirds of our population—a development our society has not yet faced up to. The closest Soviet parallel appears to be the class preference given to the children of "workers." This preference was originally said to be justified as a correction constant for the cultural decrement in their measures of intellectual competence. But the term "worker" has come to have a rather limited and meretricious meaning in Soviet society. It is used to refer particularly to factory workers and to those officials who represent themselves as identified with them. Thus what was once an equalizing factor in student selection appears to have become a distorting factor. Whether this distortion is as great as our own growing distortion, which tends to restrict higher education opportunities to the economically more privileged families, is hard to tell. In any case, I suspect the source of their distortion may be harder to dislodge than ours, for theirs has a built-in feature, via communist dogma, that up to now we have not had in our concept of democracy.

What will happen, however, if we decide that our society does not have *democracy* as its central concept, as some leaders are now suggesting, but has instead, *capitalism,* or something of that sort, as its central theme, is another matter. However defensible

tions of this complex matter, and besides, they involve dimensions of Soviet life that I cannot, at the present time, unfold to my own satisfaction.

One other fact, which is not so generally known, is that each year the Soviet Union publishes about four times as many new books as the United States—the next most productive country in the publication of this form of literature. With this tremendous publication list they not only seek to satisfy the voracious demand of Soviet citizens for serious reading material, but they make much needed educational materials available for underdeveloped countries. That these educational materials have a communist slant and put the Soviet Union in an unrealistically favorable light, goes without saying. But, more important than this, they constitute tangible evidence abroad of the Soviet Union's commitment to universal education, free of cost to all persons. This commitment stands very close to the center of the Soviet system, more so, I am now convinced, than does any such commitment in our society.

We visited a bookstore in Leningrad a few days after entering the Soviet Union. It was a beehive of activity. Indeed, it was the only instance of merchandising we saw where the demand appeared to be in excess of the supply. We saw no such throngs in the gastronomes—grocery shops—in the department stores, or even at the theater box offices. In the bookstore we observed the types of books being bought. They were serious books, not murder mysteries or comic books such as one sees displayed at most American bookstands. There were books on mathematics, electronics, history, political science, economics, and geography. The bookstores have a practice of accepting used books as partial payment for new ones, with liberal trade-in allowances. Thus it appears likely that a considerable proportion of the new books published each year are read by more than one reader.[4]

It was not an uncommon sight on a Moscow bus, at the end of a working day, to see begrimed laborers reading technical books which, if the illustrations I could see over the men's shoulders were any indication, were quite advanced. When we were in the Moscow airport waiting for the jet plane to take us to Tbilisi, news arrived that astronaut Gagarin was in orbit. During the flight to

---

private capitalism may be, or however broadly we define **it,** there is nothing in the concept that is likely to serve as grounds for making education equally available to all. We shall have to see how the American society's image of itself develops during the next ten years. And it will be equally important to watch for new developments in Soviet society, too. Such is the central psychological significance of the cold war.

[4] This was in Leningrad, of course, which is still Russia's "window to the West." Probably no other city in the Union is as interested in the horizons that lie beyond the drabness that encompasses its daily life.

Tbilisi we received frequent bulletins, concluding with the bulletin that he had safely landed. There was applause and excited conversation, both in the Moscow airport and on the plane. But I noticed that between the flurries of activity two of the men in front of us returned to the books they were reading. One of the books had illustrations of complicated wiring diagrams and pages of mathematical equations. I couldn't see the other one.

Now here we have some observational evidence of the viability of the construct we have been tracing in such detail. The pursuit of learning is not merely a legalized opportunity or a perfunctory ritual, it is a daily fact—a way of life demonstrated by individuals left to the impulse of the moment. It represents a dimension of human freedom which is used, not merely talked about.

Nations and the Shape of Things to Come

In terms of these everyday goings-on one cannot help but draw comparisons between the meaning of education in the Soviet Union and its meaning to those of us who take it for granted, or who take as little of it as is necessary for a college degree. There is no question but that education is a tenet of our political philosophy and an important fact of our economy. It has been so ever since a century ago when Horace Mann uttered his dictum that "Education is the chief defense of the nation," and was accused of being a communist for his advocation of free public schools. But in addition to this formalized position in America, what part does education play in the way we live? What does it mean, for example, to have our universities rated in terms of their football teams instead of their scholarship?[5] What does it mean in terms of such little things as what one reads on the way home from work, the choice of a television program, or the conversation between two young people in the corner drug store?

To be a valid element in a decision matrix a construct must also have visible

---

[5] This is not to imply that sports fail to play an important part in Soviet life. One of our group discussions at the Psychological Institute of the Georgian Academy of Sciences had to be cut short because of the intersectional football game scheduled that afternoon. Crowds had begun to gather at the stadium in the late morning, just as they do in an American university town. The Republic of Georgia was playing the Republic of Lithuania, one of the Baltic countries overrun by the Soviet Union and lying some 1300 miles to the northwest. But sports are sports and not a dog-wagging tail of higher education. Nor does one sense the tension when sports are discussed that he senses when the subject of universal education is brought up by a "capitalist" from America.

implications for the future. So let us ask that question, too. Does all this fascination for book learning betray a weakness in Soviet moral fiber and a fatal inability to envision the solid, neon-lighted values of our God-fearing economy? Or is it a portent of unfamiliar things to come? And what on earth do you suppose will be the outcome of another thirty years of their society going their way, and our society going ours? These are not detached, academic speculations. They are brutally realistic questions that should not require too much imagination to answer. And, to come back to our central theme, I don't believe these are questions that can be satisfactorily answered in motivational terms.

At this point I feel impelled to reiterate a point which may already be clear enough. I have been talking about one construct dimension of the decision matrix of the Soviet way of life. It is an important one, but not the only one. While it provides a clear enough picture of a road along which Soviet society may now march or retreat, there are other constructs which are important because they channel behavior in other directions, and some that are important because of their absence. A more accurate statement of how the Soviet citizen of the future will live, or what the comparative positions of Soviet and American cultures will be thirty years from now, would certainly require the delineation of more than one of the components of the decision, matrices within which the two societies function.

The Dread of Understanding Man Too Well

Now let me do something else, while certain thoughts are fresh in our minds. You will recall that earlier in this paper I invited your attention to the fact that the understanding of human behavior could be threatening. Because of this I suspected that we often employ motivational terms in order to manage human behavior without having to understand it. I suggested, furthermore, that when one comes to understand another person, there are likely to be irreversible changes iii his own personality.

It is this imminence of change within ourselves that gives the experience of threat its peculiar feeling quality. There is the sense that our faith is about to be undermined, as, indeed it may well be undermined. For any bold venture into human understanding leaves the wreckage of sacred ideas in its wake. Once we are caught up in this enterprise, the immediate prospect of what we are about to witness may even make us angry, or, if we must avoid the raw experience of anger at any cost, it may lead us to dismiss what we see as merely some evidence of obscure "motivation."

And here is the crucial point of what I am trying to do at this juncture of my discussion of decision matrices: If I have portrayed vividly enough the Soviet construct of private capitalism *versus* individual opportunity, some of you will personally have experienced the kind of threat I have been talking about—experienced it right here and now. Perhaps some of you found yourselves apprehensive in the face of the threat of a new understanding, or was it a shadow of despair that crossed your mind? Possibly some of you were angry at what you interpreted to be my lack of faith in the present posture of America, and some equally angry because the 19th Century promise of this great democracy has been so widely betrayed by 20th Century abuse of the freedoms it guaranteed. These were risks I took when I ventured to lift a corner of the Iron Curtain ever so slightly to give you a first hand glimpse of what lies behind. Finally, some of you may have been simply annoyed that so elusive a matter as human values should be dragged into a scientific symposium. If any of you has actually experienced these reactions, then you surely must know by now that it was not just wild speculation when I said that the prospect of understanding human behavior in other than motivational terms can be deeply threatening.

Now I must hasten on, for there remains a great deal more to be told before this paper fulfills its promise to deal with Europe's decision matrices. All that I have said so far has been my effort to disabuse you of any inclination to think in terms of motives, to paint for you a compellingly vivid picture of one alien personal construct, and to alert you to the way your own feelings are likely to become embroiled the moment you decide to join me in this quest. If you can escape from motivational habits of thought, and if you can retain both the picture and the stabilizing introspective mood I have tried to create, then what I have yet to say should make good psychological sense.

II. MATRIX DIMENSIONS

On the morning of June 9th, 1960 my wife and I boarded United Airlines Flight 610 at the spanking new air terminal in Columbus, Ohio. We were about to start a journey that would take us around the world and bring us face to face with people in 37 countries. My pocket was sagging with a two-inch-thick packet of tickets that were good for one year, and we were determined not to miss a single day of the adventure they promised us. The last entry on the last ticket read, "Chicago to Columbus, 5:10 P.M., June 8th, 1961"—we had allowed ourselves only seven hours to spare!

Every article in our suitcases had been selected, tested, weighed, and evaluated with the greatest of care, for not only had we to be prepared for arctic cold and tropical heat, but each of us must also stay within the economy class baggage limit of 44 lbs. And, besides, we had to find room within that limit for a typewriter, a tape recorder, and special color films for the camera that dangled around my neck. During the year we were to pack and unpack those bags on the average of every 3.2 days, and take them across an international boundary on the average of every five days. I must admit that our overcoat pockets bulged suspiciously, for there were some additional articles that seemed essential for our undertaking, such as the International Directory of Psychologists, that would have tipped the airport scales over our allowance. Over the great distances we were to fly any excess charges would have wrought havoc on a delicately balanced budget.

This once-in-a-lifetime argosy had been more than a year in the planning. There had been moments when it had all seemed like a child's phantasy; it could not really happen. And there had also been some chilling moments when it seemed that indeed it could not happen, for shortly after the original plans were laid I had an acute coronary attack that immobilized me for several months. But, for once, the p-values, against which all psychologists must gamble their scientific careers, could be ignored. The administrators of The Human Ecology Fund, without whose assistance the project would have been quite impossible, were patient, and time, that persistent meddler in human affairs, decided to play on our side. And so, on that bright June morning, when we mounted the ramp and turned to wave to the members of Our family who had come to see us off, we realized at last that this was no dream.

Lemcke's Questions

There had been some intensive psychological preparation for this undertaking. We had prepared ourselves, my wife and I, to ask some provocative questions and, what seemed even more important, to listen in certain ways. Dr. Frances Lemcke, also with the assistance of The Human Ecology Fund, had developed some group discussion procedures which we had pretested. We hoped that the use of these procedures would enable us to reach a first approximation of some of the important international decision matrices, as well as to hit upon a more sure-fire way of making such assessments.

Actually, Dr. Lemcke's procedure was only one of six approaches that we came to use, and, while it was relatively informal as psychological procedures go, it was the most elaborate, the most difficult to apply, and altogether the most fruitful. Let me describe it first.

We envisioned small groups, comprising three to fifteen persons, who might be willing to let us influence the course of their conversation for an hour or two. Since we wanted to see how they construed issues, rather than asking them to choose between alternatives we might propose, it was important that the questions with which we initiated the discussion should be more suggestive of a topical area than that they would be precise or objective. Moreover, we wanted as much as possible to put our friends in the position of asking each other questions and of seeking themselves the clarification of each other's responses. The more they interrogated each other the better would be the final statement of the issues as they saw them. After all, it was their system of personal constructs we were seeking to understand, not how they might inadvertently trap themselves within the web of our own dimensional scheme.

There were six lead questions in Lemcke's group discussion plan— the result of nine months' exploration within the American context. In Europe I often took the liberty of altering them somewhat. My entry questions usually ran somewhat as follows:

1. In your country how do people such as yourselves come to choose to become psychologists (philosophers) (psychiatrists) (social scientists)?

2. In each person's life it appears that there are points at which major lifetime decisions must be made. In this country what are the typical personal decisions that people such as yourselves must make, aside from the choice of a profession?

3. Many people in the world today are concerned about the possibility of a major catastrophe—an atom bomb perhaps, a collision of the earth with some celestial body, a devastating earthquake, or something of that sort. Suppose there should be such a catastrophe in this country, destroying perhaps half the population, half the transportation, half the buildings, etc. What would the typical psychologist do?

4. A few months ago I was sitting in a room with three of my colleagues. I allowed myself to have a phantasy about these three persons and myself. I thought, "Suppose these three individuals were stranded on an ice floe and I were a helicopter pilot sent to rescue them. The helicopter will hold no more than three persons, including the pilot, all four of us are capable of flying it, the ice floe is breaking up, and there is no possibility of making a second trip. What would I do? Suppose the typical psychologist in your country were confronted with a similar problem. How would he go about solving it? If you wish, I can describe each of my colleagues, since I know them well. However, you will have to tell me exactly what you need to know about them.

5. Here is a question involving even more phantasy. Suppose each of us were to be taken to another planet and told that we would be allowed to return to earth only if we chose to be some kind of animal. We know, of course, that certain animals are regarded quite differently in various cultures and that the attributes ascribed to animals often represent important national values. What kind of animal do you suppose the typical psychologist in your country would choose to be?[6]

---

[6] This is essentially one of the questions used by the Spanish psychiatrist, Pigem (1949) in his examination of children.

6. One more question: Suppose about twenty years from now another American psychologist were to come here and ask the same questions of a similar group of your countrymen. How do you suppose the answers might be different after twenty years?

No one could claim that simple categorical answers to these six questions would throw much light on constructs or on construct systems. For this kind of insight it is necessary to probe much deeper in order to develop statements of the alternatives among which the group envisioned its choices being made. For example, to the question about how psychologists in their country came to choose their profession, the first round of replies usually represented some effort to explain the choice in motivational terms. Now I have no particular objection to other people's explanation of their behavior in motivational terms, if those are actually the terms in which they think. But I have serious doubts that many of us actually make our decisions in such terms. I have, instead, the distinct impression that motivational terms injected into this kind of discussion serve only to make one's behavior appear rational, or, if not rational, at least psychological, and therefore, for whatever it is worth, coherent.

Constructs Underlying Occupational Choice

But there were several things one could do to clarify the underlying constructs behind the choice of psychology as a vocation. For example, most of the replies to this question had to do with the person's own choice, rather than the choice of the "typical psychologist." It was appropriate to ask, therefore, against what alternatives was the choice made. What vocational opportunities did the person abandon when he chose to be a psychologist? And on what issues was the decision finally made? What occupations did he see as standing in particularly sharp contrast to the group of occupations he had considered favorably—contrasting occupations especially to be avoided? Could he generalize the similarities and contrasts he had mentioned; that is to say, could he express the theses and their corresponding antitheses? To what extent did the group see this set of constructs operative in the vocational choice of other psychologists they knew?

As I suspect you have already begun to surmise, the wealth of information accruing from this method of inquiry was far greater than one could hope to report in a single paper. Not only did construct dimensions begin to appear, but other things as well—frustrations, compromises, stubborn hopes for the future, disillusionments, despair, conflicts between social groups and between economic groups, impatience with entrenched professors or university policies—all of the overtones of a complex decision matrix. Still, the important outcome of our inquiry was the dimensions themselves—the system of alternatives these persons conceptualized, and therefore the only pathways psychologically available to them. These, by the way, are the ultimate dimensions of human freedom. No others can be of any human use!

Constructs and Personal Freedom

Perhaps at this point I should take a moment to illustrate how personal construct dimensions open up pathways of freedom in what otherwise may seem to be a deadlocked situation. During our visit to the Institute of Psychology in Moscow one of the psychological assistants employed in the Institute was assigned to us as a translator. She was an attractive little girl, very serious, conscientious in her choice of technical words, but quite expressive in her inflection and gesture, and with a manner of relating herself to people that was both open and ingenuous. How had she come to choose psychology as a vocation?

First of all, she did not wish to be a psychologist; her long-standing ambition was to become an actress—a serious actress. But the University of Moscow budgets the support it gives to students according to the faculties in which they study and according to an appraisal of needs of the Soviet society. In her case she had been unable to secure support for her study of dramatic arts, but, being a bright student, could qualify for support in other fields that were more heavily subsidized. As she examined her objectives more closely she was able to conceptualize a relationship between psychology and dramatics. She proceeded to qualify herself in psychology, completed the psychology curriculum, and found employment in the Psychological Institute.

She had also studied English, both as preparation for a career as an actress and as a skill considered highly valuable in the Soviet Union, especially wherever psychological research is carried on. Moreover, the Institute was downtown on the old university campus, close to the city's theater activities. Having established herself as a full-time research psychologist, with useful language skills and the responsibility for interpreting the ideas and feelings of English-speaking people, she was free to study drama in the evening, also a task of interpreting the ideas and feelings of characters who might not otherwise be properly understood.

At first glance her record might be regarded as no more than the result of a compromise within a rigid system that denied her the freedom she would have liked to have. But it was much more than that; she did not sell so much of her time to the Institute merely in order to earn the money to do what she wanted in the hours that remained. She reconceptualized her objectives, rather than compromised them, and by putting them in a different perspective established a decision matrix for herself that permitted her to move ahead with a minimum of artificial compromise and a maximum of intellectual integrity. She was not merely "putting in hours" and "earning money" in the Institute; she was training herself in the art of interpreting human behavior. Thus she was fulfilling her life rather than subjecting it to economic circumstances. She was no less of a psychologist than the other research workers in the Institute, and scarcely less of a student of the theater, I dare say, than the others who shared her evening classes. She had thought through a dimension of life and, in doing so, had found a measure of freedom in a society where personal freedom is not easy to come by.

And may I say just one more thing while I am about it—just to forestall any tendency some of you may have at this moment to lapse back into motivational thinking. I don't think the intensity of this young lady's motivation, assuming there is any such thing for a person to have, had anything to do with what she was doing. If there had been nothing but a burning desire to be an actress the temptation would have been, not to conceptualize, but to compromise. She would have sold herself to the best-paying job she could find, saved every kopek, hated herself all day long, daydreamed of the stage, and come alive only in those stolen moments she could spend at the theater

Other Approaches

So far, I have described only one of the approaches my wife and I employed—the Lemcke Series—and, for the most part, I have been speaking of the first question only in that series, the question about vocational choice. Since this first question served mainly to initiate the discussion at a practical level, and generally did nor involve as much abstraction as the five subsequent questions, you can readily see that I am having to leave out some of the most important parts of the methodology.

More often than not it was impossible to assemble a group for the kind of discussion the Lemcke approach envisioned. Even when a group was assembled, it was not always feasible to press them into this kind of conversation. In some instances, as in Denmark, for example, it was obvious that the group, assembled around the table in a home and under the most convivial circumstances, was less than enthusiastic about any-thing that smacked of a psychological inquiry. In some instances I found that we were members of a group that wanted to ask questions about psychology in America or about my own theoretical stand in psychology. Often I found myself limited to what could be learned in a conversation with one or two persons during a half hour's visit across a professor's desk.

As it turned out, we found ourselves using essentially six types of approaches, or combinations of them, depending on the circumstances or the mood of our hosts. The first, and most elaborate, was the group discussion based on Lemcke's questions, which I have already sketched. The second group method, used most effectively in places such as Prague, Warsaw, and Moscow, was a lecture given at the invitation of the local university or academy of science people, and dealing with personal construct theory. These lectures were usually followed by lively discussions lasting until late in the evening. There were also some occasions when I was asked to describe American graduate training in psychology. These naturally led us to problems of decision-making for psychologists and others in similar occupations. Some information could be gleaned from discussions of local research projects, since the laboratory walk is a standard part of any psychologist's visit to another university.

Where friendships developed beyond the formality of the initial visit, the conversation often turned to wartime and immediate post-war experiences. Most Europeans have vivid memories of this catastrophe, for the last war affected civilians in unprecedented ways that are hard for Americans to envision. For most Europeans their recollections of wartime experiences are tightly bound to their construction of life and any discussion of these traumatic events is likely to lead to some kind of effort to structure and evaluate the course of human affairs.

Finally, there was a question I found particularly useful when I was limited to a brief visit with men in their offices, in their laboratories, or at the lunch table. It ran like this: "I am impressed with the rapid changes that are going on in Europe these days. Undoubtedly these are going to have far-reaching consequences in your country as well as in others during the next decade or so. What roic do you scc psychologists, or the science of psychology, playing in the developments that lie ahead?"

The answers to this question varied greatly from country to country and in ways that seemed reasonably representative of the prevailing decision matrix. In Norway, for example, the young psychologists saw psychology as a major dynamic factor in the new society they believed to be emerging, while in Austria the answer was a flat, "none"—an answer reminiscent of the prewar German intellectuals' disclaimer of any responsible part in the ominous course of events leading up to the Nazi tyranny.

Ways to Listen

As I have already said, as much depended on the ways my wife and I listened as on the ways we posed questions. As a matter of fact, asking and listening must go together, for the act of asking a question attunes one's ear to the sort of answer he expects, and one usually asks his questions in the light of what he thinks he has heard.

Basically, personal construct theory ought to alert one to the implied similarities and contrasts in a respondent's use of terms or in his descriptions of events. If two incidents are described in the same context, one examines both content and syntax to detect, if he can, what the speaker sees as similar between them, and in what way he sees them in contrast with each other. These similarities and contrasts are the traces of the construct dimensions being used. The incidents mentioned are the operations designating the poles of these constructs and hence serve to define them by what is known in logic as the method of extension.

Often the contrasts are clearly implied by the use of introductory phrases in sentences, as, for example, when a sentence is introduced by the phrase, "In *this* country . . . " or *"Our* students are. . . . " It is clear that what follows in the sentence is believed by the speaker to stand in contrast to something he thinks is true in some other country, or of another group of students. Often the speaker is distinguishing between what is true of his country or of his students and what he believes to be true of America or of American students, although the context of the conversation may suggest that he has some other contrast in mind.

Indeed, almost anything that a person chooses to say in a conversation may be regarded in either of two ways; a further elaboration of something that' has just been said or of something the presence of his listener implies to him, or, on the other hand, it may be regarded as a statement having salience; that is to say, something that stands out in clear contrast to what has just been said by others, or distinguishes itself from what the listener is believed to represent. To catch the full meaning of what is being said, therefore, one must not limit his listening merely to an absorption of the content or to following a sequence of images, no matter how vivid they may be. He must alert himself to the construct dimensions which serve to conjoin and separate the elements of the conversation. Without such structuring dimensions a conversation would be no more than a kaleidoscopic succession of images.

In an ordinary conversation a speaker will go over and over the same construct dimensions, varying the content, from time to time appearing to change the subject, and approaching the same dimension of thought or feeling, first at one pole and then at the other. One soon senses, if he tries, that the speaker is trying to impress an abstract meaning on his listener by continually shifting its concrete underpinnings. It is up to the listener nor to limit himself to stringing these bits of information on his own most convenient axes of reference, but to attempt to abstract from what is being said the true axes of the speaker's system.

There is an axiom often useful in psychotherapeutic interviewing: *The patient may readily change the subject, but only rarely does he change the theme.* In fact, it is by tracing the theme from subject to subject that the therapist gradually distills what is pervasive from what is merely illustrative. This is precisely what one must do in listening to any conversation if he is to detect its underlying essentials. Yet the illustrative material is often so shocking or so dull that the listener becomes preoccupied with it and fails to comprehend what is of central importance.

At a more technical level I might mention listening for the "buts," the "on the other hands," and the "therefores." These are obvious signs of contrasts and linkages. One can look for synonymous usages of terms. He can be alert to compounded modifiers of nouns, chains of modifiers, sweeping generalizations, and name-calling, all of which are common features of propaganda and are therefore likely to carry loose personal meanings which are quite remote from the dictionary meanings of the words used. He can make note of distance-making modifiers; "that versus this," "they versus we," "that class of people," etc. He can he aware of terms that seem to serve more as signals than as conveyors of semantic meanings— "the Germans," "the Nazis," "the Fascists," etc. Here again there *may* be evidence of a generalization which the person is not prepared to break down into its component parts.

It is often important to watch for artificial breaks in the chain of conversation, for interruptions by other members of the group, for sudden silences, for breaks in a line of discussion to ask the listener a question. There may be sudden blockages in the fluidity of the discussion, or inferential leaps that leave obvious logical gaps in the chain of reasoning, or there may be frantic efforts to disengage from a topic altogether. These are clues to the possibility that the contrasting pole of the construct is threatening and to the fact that the speakers are reluctant to disclose it.

One looks for areas in which discussion is spontaneous and where spontaneity breaks down. He observes constructs where one pole is discussed freely but the contrasting pole is avoided. There are likely to be some matters brought up when one is alone with the speaker which are never mentioned when a third person is present. This is particularly true behind the iron curtain. We were somewhat surprised to discover that constructs underlying such surreptitious conversations are likely to be fairly clearly expressed. In some cases there may be over-documentation of certain conclusions. This suggests that the speaker has some apprehension regarding the antitheses of those conclusions.

Who and Where

In planning this preliminary study of Europe's decision matrices, we had to make some decisions about sampling. We were less concerned with reaching a final statement regarding the decision matrix of a given country than we were about testing the feasibility of the methods derived from personal construct theory. Any final formulation of a particular decision matrix would have to be based on extensive experience within a single country, with proper regard for subcultures, for sizes of samples, and the rate at which patterns were changing. Furthermore, to concentrate on one country alone in our survey, would have led us to become overly involved with the similarities and contrasts between that country and our own. It seemed that only by maximizing the differences between the national cultures we visited that we could hope to get a proper perspective on our method and to determine whether or not it might be expected to reflect major cultural differences.

But we wanted to do something else, too, partly from tile standpoint of convenience and partly from the standpoint of methodology. Obviously our most ready access to persons abroad was through our identification with a university and with the discipline of psychology. The fact that my own psychological interests at the present time are largely theoretical also provided a rather broad meeting-ground for conversations with psychologists abroad. Psychologists throughout the world know a good deal about each other, and university people, regardless of discipline and nationality, are likely to sense a common bond among themselves. We, therefore, had what was more or less a ready-made access to universities in general and to psychologists in particular.

But even without this common interest in psychology, it would have been desirable to concentrate the study upon a particular kind of subculture. We were not seeking to distinguish the decision matrices of classes, but of national groups. It is to be assumed that the differences between socio-economic classes reflect distinctive differences in decision matrices. Indeed, one of the primary ways in which socio-economic classes are identified by sociologists is in terms of privileges, which are certainly closely related to the freedom of action within a kind of decision matrix. While I believe there is a lot of stereotyped nonsense in the unidimensional way social scientists talk about classes— "upper lower class," "lower middle class," and all that sort of thing, there are, nonetheless, sub-cultural differences worth taking into account. In making our plans it therefore seemed desirable to keep to the same type of subculture as we moved from country to country in our effort to become sensitive to national differences.

Now I suspect it may be true that the differences between psychologists from country to country are less remarkable than the differences between other types of sub-culture — merchants, for example, or perhaps miners. From this point of view our methodology is open to valid criticism. But I am not sure we can tell a *priori* what these sub-cultures are in which we may find greater national differences reflected.

There was a third reason for choosing to talk mostly to psychologists. We were trying out a set of psychological techniques and our target was a psychological problem. It was therefore possible to discuss frankly with our respondents just what we were doing and to enlist their comments on the spot. Psychologists tend to be pretty articulate people and we were often grateful for the opportunity to discuss with them just what we were trying to accomplish.

I should point out that our discussions were not limited to psychologists. There were often philosophers in our groups, as well as sociologists, psychiatrists, and individuals from other disciplines, who had a personal ancillary interest in the behavioral sciences. I should mention also the fact that we had very little contact with Americans during our year abroad. We did not mingle with embassy people, with military or technical assistance people, or with tourists, except on rare occasions, and then only briefly. In other words, we concentrated on psychologists and people like them and saw very little of "The American Community" in cities we visited. In some ways, I suppose, this was a disadvantage, but we thought, everything considered, it was best to maximize our contacts with foreign friends.

Altogether, then, our sampling specifications were simple enough: Concentrate on Europe, maximize national differences, and minimize sub-cultural differences by sticking to university communities and talking to psychologists and their friends. We did, of course, have a good many contacts outside university communities and with persons in nonprofessional occupations. But our very tentative observations in these cases are not part of the study I am reporting.

A Scandinavian Construct

While the differences in national outlook among the five Scandinavian countries (Denmark, Finland, Iceland, Norway, and Sweden) are often surprisingly great, there is one construct dimension which stands out in their appraisal of international affairs. Scandinavians, partly because of their relatively high standards of living and their high level of literary activity, often visit the United States and take keen interest in comparing their way of life with ours. The Finns, because of the unique system of fellowships for study in the United States operating over the past forty years, are particularly alert to similarities and differences between their society and ours. Their friendship for America runs deep. This seems to be especially true among university people. While the Finns were defeated in two wars occurring in rapid succession, in one of which they found themselves aligned against us, and while they have been and are still being systematically plundered by the Soviet Union, our erstwhile ally, they have made an amazing recovery Some measure of that recovery can be attributed to the leadership of persons who had training in the United States.

The Danes and the Norwegians have had particularly close contact with us since the war, and Americans who travel abroad are likely to agree that there is no place in Europe where an American feels more comfortable and accepted than in the homes and on the streets of Copenhagen. The story is somewhat different in Sweden, where local scholars feel they have been cut off from America because of their country's refusal to join NATO. It is painfully different in Iceland where the presence of Americans is regarded as akin to a military occupation. Our activities are deeply resented there, even though they are conceded to be a necessary safeguard against Soviet aggression.

All this contact with America leads Scandinavians to attempt some sort of generalization of the differences they see between their way of life and ours. It is a generalization that appears to arise spontaneously among individuals, rather than following from some official ethnocentric line.

Probably the most shocking thing a Scandinavian sees when he visits the United States is the unbelievable squalor of our cities, towns, and countryside. However he may be impressed with our highways, our universities, and our productive capacity—and he is indeed impressed by these things—he carries away with him a sickening image of the abject hopelessness of the less privileged fourth of our population—of Negroes living in despair, of dilapidated farms, of mental hospitals that look like mismanaged zoos, of fear and violence stalking our city streets, of prisons and courts that have little relation to impartial justice or to the restoration of self-respect, an image of the sick and the helpless being stripped of their dignity the moment they are driven to seek aid. Alongside this he sees profligate spending, arrogant expense accounts of men in private industry, the poor being taunted because of their poverty, and wealth flaunted in the face of the needy. He hears Americans in comfortable surroundings extolling something they call private enterprise in the midst of an economy that has obviously been taken over by corporate enterprise, and he hears of the virtues of self-reliance from people whose fortunes were handed down to them. He wonders why, in a country where self-reliance is regarded so highly, there are so many who seem to have given up in despair and, where equality is so often talked about, there are so many who have no part to play. He concludes that in America it is a disgrace to be colored, to be poor, to be a child without parents, to be sick after you have spent your last dollar on doctor bills, or to be old and helpless.

Almost without exception lie is deeply shocked by what he sees, and particularly so because he likes the Americans he meets, and is unfailingly impressed by their courtesy, hospitality, and personal generosity to him. Yet there are few Scandinavians now who do not think of America as the grand contemporary example of extremes of wealth and poverty—not the extremes of a five per cent wealthy against a ninety-five per cent impoverished, but the extremes of a three-fourths self-righteously successful against a one-fourth contemptibly derelict. Against what he sees and hears here the Dane or the Swede cannot help but draw contrasts from his own country and the responsibilities its citizens feel incumbent upon them; for none of the things I have mentioned among his observations could easily be said of a country like Denmark or Sweden, not even if one takes into account a certain amount of poverty to be found there.

I suspect this is a point where I would be well advised to ask you to recall just what it was we were attempting to do. Our task—remember—was, and is, to examine the decision matrices of Europe and to clarify as best we can the construct dimensions in turns of which the people of Europe do what they do and stand prepared to do whatever it is they will do in times of national emergency. The particular construct I have been delineating is not typically an American construct; few Americans see their society, or other societies, in terms of this dimension. And, furthermore, as if it were not abundantly obvious during the last few minutes, may I remind you that looking through other people's glasses is hard on the eyes. Is anyone for changing the topic back to something more academic—such as "motivation?"

Idealism and Materialism

During our visits to university cities it was a simple matter to stop by bookstores in the student districts and observe what books were being displayed and bought. We were surprised in many instances to find what a large proportion were American books. In Helsinki, for example, a rough check indicated that about half the textbooks displayed were American, with the remainder distributed among Finnish, Swedish, British, and German titles. The topics ranged from science to history and literature. I expressed this surprise to a group of Finnish university people one day and was rewarded by an enlightening reply from these astute observers of world affairs who survive under the shadow of the Soviet Union only by intensive research in political science and keeping their wits about them from week to week.

While Finnish authors are reputed to publish more books in proportion to the population than do those of any other country in the world, except perhaps Iceland, they were, up until the beginning of the last war, greatly dependent upon German textbooks. Like many other people, they looked to Germany as a fountainhead of both science and literature. America, by contrast, was the country where automobiles, airplanes, movie stars, illiterate millionaires, and addle-headed tourists came from. To a somewhat similar extent this axis of German scholarship versus American simple-minded materialism structured the thinking in other countries of Europe as well.

But there has been a curious shuffle since the wan The same construct dimension still holds, but America and Germany have exchanged positions. Now it is the Germans who are the materialistic, money-conscious, crude-mannered, vulgarians of the world, and it is the Americans who are exporting scholarship. German economic growth has been spectacular while American economic growth seems on the point of grinding to a halt. Reactionary voices call America back, not to the dynamics of the nineteenth century but to the status of the nineteenth century, not to the forward look of our pioneers, but the backward look of those who keep talking about them. Since the war we have displayed a strange inability to get things done or to implement any programs comparable to Europe's Common Market. More and more the Germans are making the world's automobiles, the Dutch its medicines, the Italians its business machines.

But when we look at the other pole of this dimension we see something that we can scarcely believe ourselves. America is exporting scholarship as no nation of modern times has ever exported it. American scientific research on a broad front is outdistancing the contributions of other countries. In almost any field you can mention American textbooks are far ahead of those available elsewhere. American artists are exhibiting and performing with exciting new style and competence. America is rapidly coming to mean scholarship and intellectual leadership. This is indeed a switch of images.

Now I have been elaborating considerably on what was actually told me that evening in Finland. This elaboration, however, is based on observations in other parts of Europe and it substantially represents, I believe, an important dimension in the thinking of social scientists in a number of countries—though certainly not in all. Moreover, I doubt if all segments of the societies in which I observed this dimension make the same use of the contrast I have described, or, if they did, if they would all see American scholarship in such a favorable light. Our study is sharply limited to preliminary observations in the kind of sub-cultures we chose to visit.

Nevertheless, I believe we have something important here. So let me go on and describe the remarkable way in which this dimension of thought has guided the affairs of nations during the last decade and a half.

German idealism has always been an important pole of Germanic thinking. While idealism might at first glance appear to be antagonistic to empirical science, it has not always worked out that way in Germany. Indeed it often supported experimentation. The logical positivists of the Vienna Circle, taking their cue from Bertrand Russell of Britain and the American pragmatists, attempted to clean house in German science and sweep out the vestiges of idealism. But German idealism was not to be junked so easily; it was instead about to assume its most grotesque form and plunge the world into a Nazi nightmare.

Germany came out of the war with its idealism discredited, both at home and abroad. How deep this sense of invalidation was is hard to say. But at least it was acute enough on the surface. In the face of such invalidation, then, what was there for the German mind to do? Certainly if one finds his position untenable he must change it, if he is to survive. But how? How do you shift your position, except to move in the most obvious direction from where you stand and along the broadest avenue your mind has been able to pave for itself? For the German, this avenue ran straight from "German" idealism to "American" materialism. What could be more obvious—and with the American occupation forces, from Army sergeants to State Department officials, to show just how it could be done!

But I must point out that such massive shifts are not made along lines that are laid down by strangers from across the Atlantic, or by the immutable logic of the universe, but along lines that are construed by the human mind itself. The idealism the German felt himself forced to abandon was not the Nazism Americans perceived, but the Nazism he himself had experienced. Nor was that idealism some island perched out in natural space, existing independently of what man perceives, it was what the German experienced it to be in his own generation. And the materialism he envisioned as the alternative now open to him was not the America we experience, but the America he perceived us to be. Hence the shift became what it was. Western Germany, and to a considerable extent Eastern Germany too, has moved toward what they and most of the rest of Europe believed was "successful Americanism!" It has made this move with some misgivings on both sides of the Atlantic, for it was not altogether in the direction of their sober convictions or of what we deeply believe.

That this move may prove to be superficial must go without saying. Indeed, Americans might fervently hope that it is superficial, and that, instead of slipping back again into the old slot toward fascism the moment the American glamor has worn off, the German mind will conceptualize some new dimensions of national life. But we should not expect too much. We must remember that while war and defeat may challenge men to find new pathways along which civilization may move, the suddenness and shock of a great catastrophe too often cause men to turn and run back along old familiar alleys.

One Man's Matrix of Decision

Thus far I have attempted to sketch only two dimensions of European cultural change—one that I have called the Scandinavian dimension of *Humanitarianism versus Opportunism,* and the other that might be called the German dimension of *Ideas versus Wealth*. Rather than going on to catalog other dimensions and trace more complex matrices— which, as you see, takes time—let me show how this simple two-dimensional matrix defines some anxious choices in the life of an individual man and how it channels the destinies of nations in moments when great decisions are made.

A few months before the Berlin wall was put up, my wife and I had the opportunity to make the acquaintance of some young university instructors in Humboldt University, the old and respected "University of Berlin." It happens that this university lies just inside the Soviet sector of the city. Since the war an impressive new university, called the Free University of Berlin, has been erected in the American sector with the generous help of American funds. But one does not construct universities simply by building buildings and recruiting a distinguished staff. In some strange way, quite apart from these important features, each university seems to have its own integrity and character. Humboldt University, though it is now plastered with communist slogans and humming with programs for communizing Latin America, still retains some of its distinction as a center of scholarship. In some of its departments professors are under continual or intermittent harassment, yet are able to carry on in some degree in the old scholarly tradition. In spite of all their handicaps their work stands out in contrast to that in corresponding departments of the Free University where all the gleaming new buildings and equipment are. Psychology is one of those departments.

During one of a number of conversations a young man spoke of the pleasure he and his wife experienced on those occasions when they could leave the darkened rubble-covered streets of East Berlin and take the 5-Bahn train over to West Berlin. He expressed himself something like this:

"Do you know, even if I were to be offered a position with higher rank and pay in another city of the People's Democratic Republic, my wife and I have agreed that we would turn it down. It would be worth the sacrifice just to be able to retain the opportunity to go to West Berlin when our spirits are ^{1}ox~ to walk the wide clean streets, to mingle with the happy crowds, to be caught up in the bright lights, and to look at the endless displays of beautiful things behind big plate glass windows. For us who live in East Berlin it is an exciting privilege just to go over there and breathe the air."

An American, hearing this kind of remark, is likely to feel a lump in his throat and sense a bond of kinship between himself and his newfound friend. I was no exception. After all, there is something about West Berlin that stands for America and its hopes for a war-chastened people, and one cannot help but be thrilled to hear this young man, reared under Nazi tyranny, scarred by combat, starved in a military prison camp, and living in the bleakness of communist oppression, speak of breathing the air of - - - Here he is, a

40

man who, in spite of all that tried to warp his life, has caught a glimpse of that dimension in which all human life seems to pulsate, that dimension so dear to the American heart.

Oppression versus Freedom!

We asked this young man, almost in our next breath, if he was planning to flee the Eastern Sector, something that at that time would have been easy enough to do. The immediate reply was, "No! Why?" The answer, with its overtones, ran something like this: "Well, the rents are very high over there—four or five times as much as we pay. To be sure there are employment opportunities now, but some day something you cannot help will happen. You may lose your position and if you lose your position in Western Germany your financial resources dwindle away very rapidly, very rapidly indeed. Before you know it, you and your wife and your children may be thrown out into the street. That sort of thing happens over there. Medical care is terribly expensive over there. The doctors like to live expensively, and if you can't pay for medical care you don't get it. No, we are going to stay right here. While the pay is poor, and the streets are dark, and you are under continual criticism if someone does not think you are following quite the correct line, still I know this: My family will always have a roof over their heads, I will always have an income, and there will always be free medical care for our children and ourselves, absolutely free—good medical care. I remember very well what it was like to be without these things, when children were deserted in the streets, and some starved while others ate. Then I look at my own children, and I know what my decision must be. No, I'm staying here. My family comes first!"

"Oh ho!" you may say. "It's easy enough to see what's wrong with this fellow. He just doesn't have the motivation. All people like him want is security, security! He expects everything to be soft and easy. He thinks the world owes him a living. He's a coward; he's afraid to face up to life. It takes a real man to enjoy freedom and he obviously doesn't measure up."

These comments are, of course, in the language of motivational psychology. They are not the sort of thing one says if he is looking for a glimpse of the world through the other fellow's glasses. They are an outsider's explanation, or, more correctly, a way of dismissing any claim this man may have to validity for the matrix of his decision. The psychology of motivation is like that!

But I have committed you to understanding this man in terms of the psychology of personal constructs. Let us, therefore, look more closely to see if we can detect the principal dimensions of his thought. He has expressed two main ideas, the first, the feeling he and his wife have when they walk the crowded streets of West Berlin, and the second his sense of over-riding responsibility to his family. The second is easy enough to understand in terms of what we called our "Scandinavian dimension of *Humanitarianism versus Opportunism.*" I-fe sees matters in terms of this issue and he chooses for himself the pole of humanitarianism, presumably, of course, with certain personal modifications of the construct.

But what about the first statement? Was it the air of "freedom" that he and his wife were breathing on those walks along the brightly-lit Kurfürstendamm— "freedom" as Americans understand it? I suspect it was not, really, just as I am sure it is not for all too many Americans. What they were breathing was the air of excitement, of glamor, of lavish wealth, of the endless display of goods—shiny things, soft things, luscious things—the air of the abundance of material possessions. No doubt they remembered something too, something that happened when they were youngsters—trumpets and flags, the quickened heart-beat that keeps time with marching feet, the spectacle of the launching of a thousand-year Reich, the power of brushing away all the villainous adversaries that fouled the path to greatness, the realization that they themselves, that they were not only Aryan but German. It has been twenty years now, but who can ever forget the bursting thrill of idealism rising in the adolescent breast.

But all that is gone now. Nazi idealism has proved itself to be cruel and wrong, and it has led to bitter reprisals from those who did not share that dream, just as all great ideals of faith, of hope, and deep conviction prove to be cruel and wrong when they are held too dearly. Ideals are as dangerous as they are powerful, and they lead to death and bitterness. One scarcely dares think of those adolescent moments now, or try to remember how he felt, much less mention such things aloud. So "idealism" is dead now. It perished with the millions of Jews it slaughtered and is buried with them in the same mass graves.

As this young man and his wife mingle with the shopping crowds in the KaDeWe, or stroll among the sidewalk diners at Krantzler's, I am sure they must hear the echo of distant drums, and sense a rising excitement. I am sure not even that dark ruined tower of the Gedächtniskirche, left standing high in the center of West Berlin's most brightly lighted district as a stark reminder of evil days, can slow the pulse or draw one's attention altogether away from the lush splendor of the Berlin-Hilton Hotel. This time it will be different. It is not the Nazi thrill one should have now, but the thrill of prosperity—like they are always talking about in America.

I have, to be sure, taken some liberty here in interpreting the personal experiences of our friends. And while I may be mistaken in some factual details, our inquiries into the dimensions of European thought lend strong support for the conclusion that one of the principal axes involved in the German's changing world is that of *Ideas versus Wealth.*

A Premature Conclusion

And now I am near the end of this paper. There were so many things I started out to say, and so few that got said. I suppose I should have fulfilled the promise of my title—The Decision Matrices of Europe—by cataloguing more of the dimensions of European thought and by suggesting what the cultural shifts may be if sudden emergencies should arise. I would like to have told you about the French, the wildest free-for-all discussion of Lemcke's questions one could ever imagine, their tolerance of intellectual innovation, their shocking proposals of standards by which to evaluate life. Or the Spanish; I would like to tell you about them, how they gracefully stalked me as a matador stalks a bull, making thrusts, stepping neatly aside, dangling false questions, until at last they were satisfied and let me hear what they were bursting all the time to say. I would like to try to make you feel that personal construct and how it bears upon the ever-approaching choice between Franco-ism and communism, a choice that might have been between Franco-ism and democracy—twenty-five years ago! Most of all, I would like to have told you about the exciting things that are happening to Marxist theory in Poland, and the wisp of hope they hold out for a more tolerant world. But the time is nearly gone, and I want to close with a little incident.

Just a few weeks after our return from the Orient last summer, my wife and I made a second trip to Europe. We met one of our East Berlin friends again. Just a few days before, the Berlin wall had gone up. No more happy walks along the Kurfürstendamm, no more neon lights, no more window shopping! At the moment we talked to *him* there was still a legitimate way to flee to West Germany, and to take his family with him. He was facing his personal matrix of decision, just as today, or perhaps tomorrow, all Europe, and many other countries of the world as well, face the matrices of decision they have erected for themselves. It was obvious that he was under considerable tension. His voice quivered at times; he sought us out as old friends; he kept looking at us as if there were a question he wanted to ask, but he knew it was one we could not answer for him. For us, of course, with our own type of decision matrix, the choice might have been considerably less difficult. But each man decides within his own matrix. Our talks, on several occasions during those days last August, were warm and friendly, and we spoke briefly of the crisis in his life. But we did not press him to disclose what his decision might be. After all, human decency sets limits to psychological inquiry, and we did not have the heart to probe the anguish of his already troubled mind.

How is it that James Russell Lowell's (1897) poem runs—"Once to every man and nation comes the moment to decide…"?

References

Bieri, J. (1961). Complexity-simplicity as a personality variable in cognitive and preferential behavior. In D. Fiske & S. Maddi (Eds.), *Functions of varied experience.* Homewood, Ill.: Dorsey.

Burke, K. (1945). *A grammar of motives.* New York: Prentice-Hall.

Clemens, S. L. (Mark Twain) (1896). The stolen white elephant. In *Tom Sawyer abroad; Tom Sawyer, detective, and other stories.* New York: Harper.

Ditzen, R. (Hans Fallada) (1933). *Little man what now* (trans. by Eric Sutton). New York: Simon & Schuster

Kelly, G. A. *(1955). The psychology of personal constructs* (Volumes 1 and 2). New York: Norton.

Kelly, G. A. (1958). Man's construction of his alternatives. In G. Lindzey (Ed.), *Assessment of human motives.* New York: Rinehart.

Kelly, C. A. (1961). Suicide: The personal construct point of view. In N. L. Farberow & E. S. Schneidman (Eds.), *The cry for help.* New York: McGraw-Hill.

Lowell, J. R. (1897). *The complete poetical works of James Russell Lowell.* Boston: Houghton Mifflin.

Papashvily, C., & Papashvily, Helen *(1945). Anything can happen.* New York: Harpen

Papashvily, C., & Papashvily, H. (1946a). *Thanks to Noah.* New York: Harper.

Papashvily, C., & Papashvily, H. (1946b). *Yes and no stories.* New York: Harper.

Pigem, 1. M. *(1949). La prueba de Ia expression desiderativa.* Barcelona: Libreria de Ciencias Medic.

* Reprinted from the 1962 NEBRASKA SYMPOSIUM ON MOTIVATION, by permission of the University of Nebraska Press. Copyright© 1962 by the University of Nebraska Press. Copyright© renewed 1990 by the University of Nebraska Press.

Snakes in Ireland
(Europe's Matrix of Decision revisited)[7]

Peter Cummins

I was surprised and honoured when Jörn Scheer asked me to look at bringing up to date Kelly's paper, *Europe's Matrix of Decision*. In this paper, published in 1962, Kelly uses his experience of a divided Berlin to reflect on the limits of psychological enquiry. I was clear therefore about the value of re-visiting this paper for a PCP conference in Berlin. I was deeply puzzled about why he had decided to ask me to carry out the re-visit. Rather than asking him directly, I tried to work it out for myself. I wondered whether it was because he knew that I could speak some German. Some of you will have had the privilege to have heard Jörn's own plenary paper at the Townsville conference on conference language (Scheer, 1996[8]). This paper began with two minutes spoken in German. I have spoken to some listeners who told me it felt like 30 minutes. I quickly realised that my German was not good enough to present a paper in German. I was reassured by Mark Twain's observation that *a gifted person ought to learn English (barring spelling and pronouncing) in 30 hours, French in 30 days and German in 30 years*. I am left with the particular guilt of writing in what Jörn refers to in his paper as "Ireland profiting from her colonial language". I must talk to Jörn about his denial of the colonial status of American and Australian. Indeed it is only *recently* that an Australian court finally decided that Britain is a foreign country. Of course I may have been asked because in a previous paper at the 3rd European conference I suggested that Briton's do not construe much about Europe. Indeed I argued that like many countries they do not construe each other adequately (Cummins, 1996[9]).

Then I got around to reading the actual Kelly paper; *Europe's Matrix of Decision* (Kelly, 1996[10]). Finally it became clear why I had been asked to write this paper. In this paper, presented to the 1962 Nebraska Symposium on Motivation, Kelly suggests several other titles. These included -

---

[7] Reprinted from Scheer, J. W. (Ed.) (2000): *The person in society – Challenges to a constructivist theory.* Giessen: Psychosozial-Verlag (29-43).
[8] Reprinted in this volume, p. 104-121 *(Ed.)*
[9] Reprinted in this volume, p. 60-63 *(Ed.)*
[10] Reprinted in this volume, p. 12-44 *(Ed.)*

The whimsical possibility of writing such a convincing paper that you would be moved to change the topic of this annual Nebraska conference to

"Snakes in Ireland".

There at last was my answer... I was being secretly challenged to write a paper about the snake population of Ireland. (For those of you who do not know, the snake population of Ireland is supposed to have been driven out by Saint Patrick who lived from 385 to 461.)

I am not aware that Kelly had any particular Irish connection except for his name... but he clearly knew his Irish legends!

He was also clearly influenced by Georgian legends. In particular he tells us about a picture in the Hermitage museum which shows a poor boy listening at the schoolroom door. He contrasts this with the American response which imagines it is normal for a boy to play hooky from school. The meaning for Georgians was that the old system was a feudal system which denied education to the people and preached capitalism. This was in sharp contrast to the emphasis of the revolution on the right of the people to education.

Kelly was clearly impressed by the Soviet emphasis on the importance of education. This lead him to observe that people on the street in Russia were reading academic texts. He took this as a concrete sign that his theory, re State values, was accepted by the people; that they accepted and lived this emphasis on education. The pursuit of learning was a dimension of human freedom which was used not merely talked about.

He goes on to point out the historical ambivalence on the same topic in the United States. Horace Mann (100 years ago) stated "education is the chief defence of the nation". Apparently Mann was accused of being a communist for his advocacy of free public schools!

Kelly goes on to ask the still pertinent question:

What does it mean for education in the US where universities are rated by football team instead of scholarship?

and then the critical question:

What do you suppose will be the outcome of another 30 years of their (soviet) society going their way and our society going ours?

He goes on to state:

*These are not detached academic speculations. They are brutally rea-
listic questions that should not require too much imagination to answer.*

So there you are, not too much imagination needed!! This challenge is of
course very similar to that posed by him for psychotherapists when he says
that a therapist should always be able to predict the next therapeutic session.
Given that too often I fail to predict what the patient will bring I suppose I
take some comfort; it is clear that no one predicted that the outcome of the
Soviet Union going their way for 30 years would be the disintegration of the
union.

However despite my relief at his failure it is clear that he really meant to try
to make such predictions.

He accepts at this stage that he has only identified one component of the
decision matrix and that more would have to be identified....

*to predict what the comparative position of Soviet and American cul-
ture will be 30 years from now.*

Is such a prediction possible? Or is it, as Kelly himself acknowledged, one of
those events which will always lie outside the range of convenience of any
construing system? Du_an Stojnov, in a comment on a draft of this paper said
that neither he nor anyone he knows had any idea that Yugoslavia would
disintegrate. Nevertheless he had to change country, culture and habits without changing where he lived.

Try it out (making such a prediction) in your own life.. particularly those of
you who have moved countries or cultures.

I left Ireland in 1973, not because of my search for snakes but because there
was then no clinical psychology training course in the republic. I left a country which was Introspective, Church dominated, and Agricultural. In this it
had changed little for 100 years

*100 years ago the shrewdest observer would have bet on Belfast's fu-
ture rather than Dublin's. Belfast was a strong, developed industry,
outward looking wealthy city; While Dublin was poor, priest ridden,
and reactionary by comparison. NOW Dublin is not only booming but
fashionable while Belfast is the Politics-ridden backwater. OUR OB-
SERVER WOULD HAVE BEEN AGHAST.* (Marr, 1999)

The Ireland I left is an Ireland which is almost unrecognisable now. Ireland is
an outward looking European country with a multiple identity (Irish, European, Catholic, Trendy); with 2 clinical psychology courses!

I do not think that there is any way that I could have predicted the level of change.. mostly driven by the development of the European union. (The most common sign to be seen in Ireland is THIS PROJECT IS PART FUNDED BY THE EUROPEAN COHESION FUND).

My failure to be able to predict Ireland's change is paralleled by Kelly's failure to anticipate the break-up of the Soviet Union. This is not very surprising.

> *The soviet union was doomed to collapse as a multi national empire. but it was an entirely different matter <u>when</u> this historical moment would happen. my feeling is that the disintegration was inevitable but the historical moment, the timing was accidental. if it had not been for a number of subjective factors-- and not just the personal feud between Yeltsin and Gorbachev--- it all could have happened thirty or fifty years later than it di"* (Starovoitova in Remnick, 1997).

So it could have been thirty or fifty years later.

With the full benefit of hindsight it is striking how little mention of nationality there is in Kelly's description of the Soviet Union, it seems clear that he accepted its fundamental unity at the time. This is not too surprising as the emphasis was on being soviet.

> *The soviet union brought together 126 different nations and tried to homogenise them, managing it only superficially... religion and language usually determine the mentality of a nation , and so there were great differences. The layer of Homo Sovieticus was extremely superficial. The thickness, so to speak of this layer was probably greater in Russia or Ukraine than in Tadjikistan, Estonia, Turkmenia, or Azerbaijan* (Starovoitova in Remnick, 1997).

Starovoitova only mentions two extra dimensions, religion and language. Stojnov (1996) identifies 9 different dimensions underlying national identity:

- *ethnic*
- *religious*
- *statism* ... the need to have independence
- *historic*
- *political philosophy* ...expansionist, integrating the people into one country
- *ideologies* ...monarchism, democracy, communism
- *superstatism* ...Other states have an interest in what happens
- *cultures* ...different ethnic groups with different religions result in different cultures
- *economic.*

The sheer difficulty of this situation is well illustrated by Stojnov (1996[11]) when he says: "Every anticipated strategy which could satisfy one side, necessarily leads to invalidation of a solution constructed by another".

He was talking about the split up of Yugoslavia but he could have been talking about much of the history of Northern Ireland.

With his example of the soviet construct of capitalism as his model Kelly set off on a year's trip around Europe. From this trip he wrote his paper called *Europe's Matrix of Decision*. This trip was delayed a year by a heart attack. I realised that this probably means that his paper *Confusion and the Clock* (1977) was written while he was on his trip around Europe. The first part of this paper was written before he had his heart attack. He then returns to finish the paper over a year after his illness. In this paper he says:

> *13 months and an ocean now separate me from the time and place at which the last of the sentences above were written.*

What is fascinating about *Confusion and the Clock* is that it itself can be read as a meditation of the nature of prediction and the question of the extent to which we can ever predict. It was to be the beginning of a book on the HUMAN FEELING - a book he never finished... it was to be a book that -

> *was not intended to prove anything; only to be an adventure in human feelings, one in which I have asked you to join me, so that, when we are finished, we can ask each other where we have been and what we have found out* (Kelly, 1977).

It shows his strong belief that the attempted to anticipate what was at the heart of his own way of life. Despite having failed to predict his own heart attack, as he puts it "The whole system of anticipation's got badly mixed up" he still strives to "look in on tomorrow". He ends this paper with a question and answer:

A. *I wonder what will happen next week*
Q. *Haven't I learned not to wonder about such things?*
A. *Oh! No! Quite the contrary!*
Q. *But won't speculation about them tend to make them happen?*
A. *Perhaps, but I insist on having some continuity in my life.*
Q. *What am I going to write about next?*
A. *Joy and depression.*
Q. *Is that to be based on experience too?*
A. *I don't know--yet !*

---

[11] Reprinted in this volume, p. 167-175 *(Ed.)*

(Confusion and the Clock, 1977)

So with this personal experience of the limits of prediction off he went.

He visited 37 countries, crossing an international boundary on average every five days. Ever the scientist Kelly went on this journey equipped with his methodologies. In all he tells us he had six different approaches. The one he intended to use most was Lemcke´s six questions:

(1) In your country how do people such as yourselves come to choose to become psychologists (philosophers) (social scientists)?

(2) In each persons life it appears that there are points at which major lifetime decisions must be made. In this country what are the typical personal decisions that people such as yourselves must make, aside from the choice of profession?

(3) Many people in the world today are concerned about the possibility of a major catastrophe - an atom bomb perhaps, a devastating earthquake, or something of that sort. Suppose there should be such a catastrophe in this country, destroying perhaps half the population, half the transportation, half the buildings, etc. What would the typical psychologist do?

(4) A few months ago I was sitting in a room with three of my colleagues. I allowed myself to have a fantasy about these three persons and myself. I thought "suppose these three individuals were stranded on an ice floe and I were a helicopter pilot sent to rescue them. The helicopter will hold no more than three persons, including the pilot, all four of us are capable of flying it, the ice floe is breaking up, and there is no possibility of making a second trip. What would I do? Suppose the typical psychologist in your country were confronted with a similar problem. How would he go about solving it? If you wish, I can describe each of my colleagues, since I know them well. However, you will have to tell me exactly what you need to know about them?

(5) Here is a question involving even more fantasy. Suppose each of us were to be taken to another planet and told that we would be allowed to return to earth only if we chose to be some kind of animal. We know , of course that certain animals are regarded quite differently in various cultures and that the attributes ascribed to animals often represent important national values. What kind of animal do you suppose the typical psychologist in your country would choose to be ?

(6) One more question: suppose about twenty years from now another American psychologist were to come here and ask the same questions of a similar group of your countrymen. \how do you suppose the answers might be different after twenty years?

The other methods were

(2) formal lecture with discussion,

(3) formal descriptions of American graduate training in psychology,

(4) the laboratory walk ... a standard part of any psychologists visit to another university,

(5) a discussion of wartime and immediate post-war experience,

(6) a final question -- I am impressed by the rapid changes that are going on in Europe these days. Undoubtedly these are going to have far reaching consequences in your country as well as in others during the next decade or so. What role do you see psychologists, or the science of psychology, playing in the developments that lie ahead?

I wonder what your own response to such a question would be. I have to admit that my own response would be a rather cynical one.. along the lines that psychology has little chance of being allowed to play any role; even if it were clear what that role should be.

I was brought up short then by his next paragraph:

> *The answer to this question varied greatly from country to country and in ways that seemed reasonably representative of the prevailing decision matrix. In Norway for example the young psychologists saw psychology as a major dynamic factor in the new society they believed to be emerging, while in Austria the answer was a flat none.....an answer reminiscent of the pre-war German intellectuals' disclaimer of any responsible part in the ominous course of events leading up to the Nazi tyranny.*

I still find this section difficult to accept. In a group discussion of it someone suggested that it reflected the role that psychology occupies in American society and an assumption that this should be true in other countries. However what it does serve to emphasise is a moral dimension of PCP. Who better to say this straight out than Don Bannister:

> *The Doctrine of superiority, whatever form it takes, is a logical articulation of the governance of the powerful over the powerless. In contrast to it, an ideal and a purpose can be attributed to personal construct theory. In the simplest possible terms, the political and psychological intent of construct theory is the total diffusion of power. Thus psychologists committing themselves to PCT, are committing themselves to those traditional, though as yet largely unimplemented, political beliefs expressed in values such as liberty, equality and fraternity.* (Bannister, 1979)

Somewhat to my amusement Kelly found that his 6 Lemcke questions simply did not work. His groups were resistant to be structured in this sort of way. Out of curiosity I have tried it twice in two different groups and had the same result, each group insisted on taking the conversation where it wanted to. I was only able to get direct answers to two questions, 1 and 5.

It was clear that there were a wide range of paths to becoming a psychologist. One person commented that in his year of British psychologists only one person's journey coincided with the approved route... and he was from India.

A religious background was a common earlier career choice for people who later become psychologists. When I have asked people to describe their journey to psychology it became clear that there is a strong thread of people who discovered they were psychologically inclined at a very early age.., e.g. one person who as a teenager asked her history teacher whether Hitler was mad, and was told that this was not a valid historical question... as far as she was concerned it was a critical question, from then on she started becoming conscious of her interest in psychological questions. I was also interested to find a background in Acting, with an emphasis on the psychological understanding of characters... parallel with Kelly's own well documented interest in acting and his description of a Russian psychology assistant and her acting career.

One group did have a go at question five:

(5) Here is a question involving even more fantasy. Suppose each of us were to be taken to another planet and told that we would be allowed to return to earth only if we chose to be some kind of animal. We know, of course, that certain animals are regarded quite differently in various cultures and that the attributes ascribed to animals often represent important national values. What kind of animal do you suppose the typical psychologist in your country would choose to be ?

Answers included:

An ant or bee... complex social system that involves poking your nose into other peoples worlds,
A meerkat... emphasising a social system which looks after each other,
A cat... independent (from Psychiatry) pretend to belong but keeps its distance, chooses who to be dependent on, leaves when it wants to,
A tortoise... needs a hard exterior even if it is mush inside.

Kelly does not tell us directly any of the answers he got from these questions. He focuses on shared constructs within particular European National groupings. He highlights two in particular, derived from Scandinavia and Germany.

The first key European dimension identified by Kelly was that of

HUMANITARIANISM vs OPPORTUNISM.

This was highlighted for him by the response by many Scandinavians to the poverty in the US:

He (the Scandinavian) carries away with him a sickening image of the abject hopelessness of the less privileged fourth of our population.

and contrasts this with "his own country and the responsibilities its citizens feel incumbent upon them"..., i.e. there is a communal responsibility for poverty in Scandinavia as distinct from the American view of poverty as personal failure.

He goes on to comment "few Americans see their society or other societies in terms of this dimension". But most Europeans would still see this as fundamental - the exception being Thatcherite politics with the famous statement "there is no such thing as society".

From Germany he highlighted

IDEALISM vs MATERIALISM.

Kelly points out how Idealism in Germany had become corru   pted to the point where it produced the NAZI party. He suggests that there was such a revulsion as a result of this that there is deep suspicion of any depth of idealism in 60's Germany... rather the switch to materialism and an emphasis on the values of a better standard of living. It is as if people were saying that it was safer and more reliable to just get on with producing a better standard of living. Ideas led to extremes.

What intrigued Kelly about this dimension was that before WW2 it had been German idealism against American materialism, since World War 2 it had become German Materialism contrasted with American Idealism. He summarises this as

GERMAN CARS vs AMERICAN TEXTBOOKS.

Kelly goes on to hope that there would be the development of some new dimensions of national life.

But we should not expect too much. We must remember that while war and defeat may challenge men to find new pathways along which civilisation may move, the suddenness and shock of great catastrophe too often cause men to turn and run back along old familiar alleys.

He reminds us of how important National Identity is. This is highlighted in his paper entitled *Man's Construction of his Alternatives*.

I have only changed one word (from introvert to Irish) in the following quote:

If I say of myself that I am Irish (introvert) - even my inner self - my self - becomes burdened with the onus of being Irish (introvert).

What has happened is that I have named myself with a name, and having done so, too quickly forgot who invented the name and what he had on his mind at the time. From now on I try frantically to cope with what I have called myself.

Moreover my family are often quite willing to join in the struggle

(Kelly 1979)

He then goes on to remind us that:

The critical question is to what extent such group consensus has on individual behaviour.. if none then the reading of the dimension of soviet life is academic and does not meet the VALIDITY CRITERIA THAT PCT REQUIRES.

At this stage Kelly tells us about a man who lives in East Berlin. This was at a time just before the Berlin Wall. The man had chosen to live in East Berlin. While he acknowledged the excitement of the west, for him the fixed rents and safe job offered by the east were more important, in other words he chose the humanitarianism of the east against the opportunism of the west.

This can be illustrated on a matrix of these two constructs:

HUMANITARIANISM

IDEALISM   MATERIALISM

OPPORTUNISM

This man liked the glamour of the wealth of west Berlin, but chose east Berlin as his family would always have a roof over their heads, he would always have an income and there would always be free medical care for his children. This was on the assumption that he would always be free to visit West Berlin to experience the "endless display of beautiful things behind big plate glass windows".

Sometime later Kelly visited Europe again just after the Berlin Wall was built. He met this man who was now struggling to decide whether to flee to the west as was still possible. He could not decide.

For us of course, with our own type of decision matrix the choice might have been considerably less difficult; but each person decides within their own decision matrix.

I wonder where he is now.. he had the practical struggle of predicting the fate of 2 countries!

Kelly himself seems to have acknowledged the difficulty of such prediction:

But at no point in history is there exact similarity with the situation in a previous age. The changes are somewhat cyclical, the path of progress would appear to follow a helix (Social Inheritance, 1979).

It is striking just how much has changed since Kelly's trip. Another example is his stating of the Spanish dilemma:

> Of the ever-approaching choice between Franco-ism and communism, a choice that might have been between Franco-ism and democracy - 25 years ago.

As previously mentioned in many regimes of the 1960's,

> considerable pressure was brought to bear by nation states to suppress anything other than an overarching national identity.

This suppression concealed what was being achieved under the surface, the underlying identities which were focused but hidden by the overarching orthodoxy... the value of a common enemy. The end of this common enemy often led to the collapse of the national identity.

The end of this national identity has in many cases led to dramatic changes in identities, e.g. the changes from being Yugoslavian to being Serbian, Croatian, Bosnian, Slovenian, Macedonian, Montenegrin, Kosovan.

What dimensions were they expressing that had been held under by previous regime? Probably at least the nine identified by Stojnov and some more. In one of the groups in which I discussed this paper the interesting question was raised of to what extent the national values identified by Kelly were in fact religious and lifestyle values, i.e. that some societies were catholic, hierarchical and rural as against more urban, less hierarchical Protestant societies.

Kelly is very conscious of the potential emotion which the discussion of identity can raise.

He was clearly worried that his audience would be threatened by his lack of faith in present American policy. He summarises this as a sense of anger because the 19th century promise of this great democracy has been so widely betrayed by the 20th century abuse of the freedoms it guaranteed.

It is indeed a subject which does raise the emotional level. Such criticism is often barely tolerated. We are all in, and construed in, a particular position.

I recently made a critical comment about the British Royal Family and was told that I was only saying that because I was Irish. When it comes to identity none of us are entirely neutral.

So what can we make of the last 30 years?

I wonder if the biggest change since the 60's when Kelly wrote this paper is the idea that a narrow sense of national identity (i.e. that I am Irish and nothing else) is a dead-end. In one of my group discussions Ray Evans suggested that the third dimension of the European matrix should be:

INSIST ON CULTURAL DISTINCTIVENESS

vs

ACCEPT CULTURAL EVOLUTION AND MIXING.

It is probably a sign of the times Kelly wrote this paper in, that his chief emphasis was on the nation state as a source of identity.

What he does not acknowledge is that many people or peoples have real problems with state identity.

This is nicely illustrated by Du Preez:

> We may construe a person's identity in terms of peripheral or even ir-relevant constructs. That is we may simply misunderstand him. We may think that his nationality or his race is the key to his identity; whereas he attaches importance to his religion, the fact that he is a good musician, and his loyalty to his family.

Du Preez goes on to point out the particular problem with national identity:

> The difficulty faced by many countries is that there is no acceptable identity to which all may be assimilated. Turk and Greek, Jew and Arab, Afrikaner and Zulu. What can they have in common? Yet why should they oppose each other.

Or: put another way:

> I have that knack of never quite fitting in, she explains. It's strange - there was no great difficulty moving countries - no more difficult than fitting in back home. I think I'm a fully integrated foreigner wherever I am (Marika Cobbold).

I can identify with this comment, as someone who is often identified as English when I am in Ireland, and Irish when I am in England. In classic family genogram terms this echoes the situation of my father's dilemma. Born in England he has lived most of his life in Ireland and has never had to decide whether he is Irish or English

This is, of course, a common dilemma. I remember being at a party near Stuttgart and someone commenting that there were only two Germans in the room. At this one responded "What do you mean two Germans? ... I am a Rhinelander."

56

A second major change since the 60's, I think, is the gradually lessening influence of the second world war. Kelly commented on this greatly affecting European identity. This is probably less true now than it was in the early sixties. This is a very difficult area since it will differ from country to country. I am particularly aware of this as Ireland was neutral, a stance which was seen as treachery in some parts of Britain. Although the influence of the second world war is much less than it was even in 1962 it is striking how often it is resorted to by British politicians and commentators, e.g. the British Defence Secretary responding to criticism of the bombing of Kosovo replied: "People would not have criticised action in Kosovo during WW2."

I am very conscious that we are now in a city[12] which is only just redeveloping its identity which has been in some ways suspended since that war.

This issue is a key one for Europe's current matrix of decision. What is to be the new European identity? In Britain it is juxtaposed; you can be British OR European but not both. There is a real fear that British identity will be subsumed by EUROPE. In some real sense Britain is seen as separate from Europe.

An English newspaper's Johannesburg correspondent wrote recently: "As I pack my cases ready to return to London I was asked are you going to Africa? The question underlines the fact that many South Africans regard the rest of their continent in rather the same way as Britons regard the rest of theirs."

The cry goes up to protect British identity. This then gets confused with the question what does it mean to be English. One of my colleagues reports her mother as saying that she had always described herself as British until moving to Wales. She was left in no doubt that she was ENGLISH.

In effect she has been forced to reconstrue her identity by the construction of Welsh--not Welsh.

I am suggesting that this paper of Kelly's can be looked at as an attempt to reflect on the whole question of Identity.

> *Where are you from?*

It is the very complexity of identity which is at the heart of our attempts to answer the central question

> *Where am I from?*
> *Who are you?*

We have moved on in some quarters to see that this question can should produce a variety of answers.

---

[12] Berlin *(Ed.)*

We end up with a new construct of

CULTURAL COMPLEXITY vs POVERTY OF IDENTITY.

Success has many ingredients but one of them, perhaps, is what you could call cultural thickness or complexity. Far from mixed identities or double languages being a handicap, they often seem to give kids more ambition, optimism, flexibility and openness. (Marr, 1999)

But can we accept this construct of Cultural Complexity without some over-all superordinate? Stojnov suggests that the only practical dimension is that of the Ethical... a formal ethical dimension calling for justice and social equality. This fits in well with Warren's (1996) conclusion that the Psychology of Personal Constructs assumes a social life in which the egalitarian outlook is prevalent. He acknowledges that there is no extant social system which encourages such an egalitarian outlook

Kelly's paper is a pioneering attempt to outline the possible contribution of PCT to the understanding of the political dimensions within which we all live. Although it reflects the limitations of its times it still contains a radical challenge for us all. I have been particularly struck by how difficult I have found it to say anything that is not rooted in my own background. In writing this paper I have been stopped many times by wondering: but would an American, German, Australian understand what this means for me; does this make any sort of sense? What will Europe be like in another 30 years? It could become the United States of Europe, stay as it is, or have a greatly enlarged European Union.

I have little or no idea what will actually happen. But then I realised that it was not for my abilities to forecast that Jörn had asked me to write this paper. The last reason that he asked me was where I am from now.

Where am I from? I now live 20 miles from Stratford on Avon, where Shakespeare came from. And as ever he had it all sorted out:

All the world's a stage, And all the men and Women merely players; They have their exits and their entrances, And one man in his time plays many parts.

References

Bannister, D. (1979) Personal construct theory and politics. In P. Stringer, D. Bannister (Eds.): *Constructs of Sociality and Individuality*. London: Academic Press.
Cummins, P. (1996) Britain after the Chunnel. In J.W. Scheer, A. Catina: *Empirical constructivism in Europe*. Giessen: Psychosozial Verlag. (*reprinted in this volume*).

DuPreez, P. (1979) Politics and identity in South Africa. In P. Stringer, D. Bannister (Eds.): *Constructs of sociality and individuality*. London: Academic Press.

Kelly, G. (1969) Man's construction of his alternatives. In B. Maher (Ed.): *Clinical Psychology and Personality*. New York: Wiley.

Kelly, G. (1978) Confusion and the clock. In F. Fransella (Ed.): *Personal Construct Psychology 1977*. London: Academic Press.

Kelly, G. (1979) Social Inheritance. In P. Stringer, D. Bannister D. (Eds.): *Constructs of sociality and individuality*. London: Academic Press.

Kelly, G.A. (1996) Europe's Matrix of Decision. In D. Kalekin-Fishman, B.M. Walker: *The construction of group realities*. Florida: Krieger. (*reprinted in this volume, 12-44*).

Lane, H. (1999). Cobbold. What more do you need; *The Observer*, London, 11th July 1999

Marr, A. (1999). Perils of ethnic purity; *The Observer*, London, 4th July 1999

Remnick, D. (1998). *Resurrection, the struggle for a new Russia*. London: Picador.

Scheer, J.W. (1996). Congress language, personal constructs, and constructivist internationalism. In B.M. Walker, J. Costigan, L.L. Viney, B. Warren: *Personal construct theory. A psychology for the future*. APS: Imprint Book. (*reprinted in this volume*).

Stojnov, D. (1996). After 40 years of peace - war in the heart of Europe. In J.W. Scheer, A. Catina: *Empirical constructivism in Europe*. Giessen: Psychosozial Verlag. (*reprinted in this volume*).

Warren, B. (1996). The egalitarian outlook as the underpinning of the Theory of Personal Constructs. In D. Kalekin-Fishman, B.M. Walker, (eds): *The construction of group realities*. Malabar,Florida: Krieger

Britain after the Chunnel[13]

Peter Cummins

When Jörn Scheer asked me to talk about Britain after the Chunnel I thought that I would have to start asking people what their constructs were about the Chunnel. The main construct I found was one of complete indifference. The possibility of a tunnel has been there for over a hundred years. The fact that it never got very far has left a sense of unreality linked to the entire project. The only strong response I got was that "you would not get me travelling in a tunnel which is over 20 miles (32 kilometres) long".

When I thought about this lack of response I realised that a tunnel is not linked to a real sense of transport. There is a very big difference between travelling around a city in the underground and on surface transport. Most underground maps are not in any sense accurate representations of the spatial layout of the city. These maps are actually highly stylised representations of the city, they bear little or no resemblance to geographical reality. As we travel around the city underground there is a lack of sense of place except insofar as different stations are architecturally distinct. This is in stark contrast to travelling over a bridge. Not far from where I live there is the Dartford crossing over the river Thames. This crossing is a tunnel travelling north and a suspension bridge travelling south. When I use this crossing I am struck by how different the two crossings are. The tunnel is a slightly unpleasant few minutes in a rather polluted atmosphere. The bridge by contrast is an adventure, crossing high over the river *but always conscious of the physical crossing over the water*. My son aged 2 and _ makes little comment about the tunnel but is clearly excited by the bridge each time we use it. When I have spoken to other people about this they have confirmed this sense of excitement and interest linked to the bridge as compared to the unreality of the tunnel.

The sheer length of the tunnel seems to be a major part of people's anxieties. We do not have constructs to deal with such an uninterrupted underwater journey. We also need to consider that the majority of people in this country who go to Europe travel to France, but no further on holiday. The common stereotype of the continent is as the source of cheap beer and tobacco. There is a central British construct that Britain is not part of Europe. This fantasy is kept going by the streetscapes/mental maps of Britain. As an Irish person

---

[13] Reprinted from Scheer, J. W., Catina, A. (Eds.) (1996): *Empirical constructivism in Europe – The personal construct approach.* Giessen: Psychosozial-Verlag (39-42).

who has lived in Britain for 20 years I am often struck by the differences between Ireland and Britain in the outward signs of belonging to Europe.

Some of the clearest examples are road signs being in kilometres in Ireland but still in miles in Britain; car registrations are now in a European model of place identification in Ireland and they often have the 12 stars of the Union on the number plate. This is quite rare in Britain. There has been a reluctant use of litres for fuel but a strong resistance to the use of litres for the measurement of any other sort of liquid! The negative images of the rest of Europe are not restricted to other countries. In Britain we have very strong constellatory preemptive constructs about other parts of Britain. Fig. 1 is one attempt to capture these constellatory constructs.

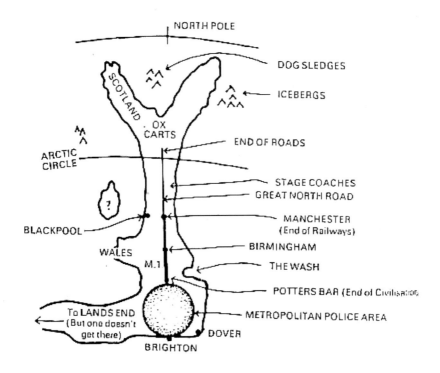

Fig. 1: *How Londoners see the North - at least, according to the Doncaster and District Development Council*

Given these difficulties it is not surprising that we have problems construing the rest of Europe!

In a recent discussion of a failed television soap opera which was set in Spain the Guardian newspaper pointed out "Brits in Spain might have stood a chance of being the basis for a workable soap, but to hurl sundry Danes, Swedes, Germans and French at the audience was to severely over-estimate the Euro tolerance of the viewing millions". In other words the British have a very limited capacity for other Europeans! It is noteworthy that in fact the quote only mentions 4 other nationalities, given that the EU is about to be enlarged to twenty countries.

When I began to try examining why this is so I was overwhelmed by hypotheses. I remember when I first trained in PCP psychotherapy that every patient displayed all constructs of transition. I have a similar problem with diagnosing Britain. I can diagnose:

Anxiety: re life after the tunnel... rabies and other diseases coming over on land... the barrier is gone and the future cannot be construed.

Hostility: Britain is not part of Europe ("Britain cannot choose which continent to belong to..." quote from British Foreign secretary).

Guilt: dislodged from the Imperial past (a politician caused uproar recently by describing Britain as "an ordinary little country").

Fear: imminent prospect of a united Europe leads to fear - it is not yet clear just how profoundly Britain would change in Europe.

Threat: Imminent awareness of change within ourselves which gives threat its peculiar feeling quality. There is the sense that our faith is about to be undermined. .as Europe becomes more prominent fear develops into threat.

Time and space do not permit me to go on. To conclude Kelly quotes Lowell's poem: "Once to every man and nation comes the moment to decide".

I cannot decide whether this moment has come yet for Britain.

An ABC* might look like this

A	*Part of Europe*	*Separate / cut off*

B	*Disadvantages*	*Advantages*
	Foreign	world power status
	ordinary country	not socialist
	not in control	special relationship with US
	medium size	

C	*Advantages*	*Disadvantages*
	civilisation	unreality
	cross cultural	poor social provision
	recognise reality	American driven

I think I show quite clearly by this where my own preferences lie!

* *Tschudi's (1977) method of eliciting positive and negative implications of the two poles of a construct (Editor's note)*

After the Wall - construct systems in united Germany[14]

Jörn W. Scheer

I should like to make some remarks on the situation of Germany before and after the Fall of the Wall that divided Berlin and the barbed wire that divided East and West Germany. They are not based on empirical research, but are personal observations.

Let's go back to Kelly first. He quotes Finnish people who up unto the last war, in his words,

> looked to Germany as a fountainhead of both science and literature. America, by contrast, was the country where automobiles, airplanes, movie stars, illiterate millionaires, and addle-headed tourists came from. To a somewhat similar extent this axis of German scholarship vs. American simple-minded materialism structured the thinking in other countries of Europe as well.

> But there has been a curious shuffle since the war. The same construct dimension still holds, but America and Germany have exchanged positions. Now it is the Germans who are the materialistic, money-conscious, crude-mannered vulgarians of the world, and it is the Americans who are exporting scholarship (Kelly, 1962, p. 115[15])

These remarks may sound more like stereotypes or stereotyped attitudes then like personal constructs. And one might feel uneasy reading statements about 'The Finns', 'The Germans', 'The Americans', 'The Scandinavians', although it is probably impossible to avoid statements like the ones mentioned.

This was in 1961, just 16 years after World War II.

At the time of Kelly's visit, it was still possible for East Berliners to visit West Berlin, to get an impression of "clean streets, bright lights, endless display of beautiful things behind big plate glass windows", as Kelly put it. Yet many people preferred to stay in the East, using a matrix of decision that comprised constructs like 'oppression vs. freedom', 'wealth vs. ideals' or 'wealth vs. social security'.

---

[14] Reprinted from Scheer, J. W., Catina, A. (Eds.) (1996): *Empirical constructivism in Europe – The personal construct approach.* Giessen: Psychosozial-Verlag (52-55).
[15] Reprinted in this volume, p. 12-44 *(Ed.)*

Thirty-three years have elapsed since! West Germany has been americanised considerably since, while East Germany has been under Soviet influence and pressure. The Communist government ruled until 1989/90. And that means, the two Germanys have developed separately for 45 years! For after 1961, only very little personal communication and exchange were possible; only few people were allowed to travel either way. Letters were controlled, introduction of books was limited, introduction of newspapers banned. I sometimes feel amazed how fast this seems to be forgotten!

How could, under these circumstances, a common culture, philosophy, national identity, even language survive? Millions of East Germans born after, say, 1940 had never travelled to the West. Hardly any West German had seen a part of the East. For Easterners, West German TV, was, hardly exaggerated, almost the only source of information on Western Europe. With this in mind, it cannot be expected that the 'commonality' of constructs, as in Kelly's corollary, was very high between West and East Germans, with the experience of life being so different!

I think it is time to become personal. Born in wartime, raised in the post-war days of shortage of everything and the subsequent cold war years, with the expectation of impending unification of Germans in the air at that time, I had different opinions and constructs about East Germany than many of my fellow country persons had. To many of the next generation, who are about thirty or younger, East Germany has been not more than one of several German speaking foreign countries like Switzerland or Austria; even more remote because of the impossibility of travelling there, and less familiar than Italy or Greece. One could say they construed these countries more like their home country than they did with East Germany.

And during the last few years, since the Cold War was nearing its end, most West Germans construed East Germany mainly as a nuisance, an annoying obstacle when driving to West Berlin on the *Autobahn*. So to many West Germans, East Germany was an uninteresting white spot on the map, and to many East Germans, West Berlin was a land of milk and honey where they could never go.

So the question arises what range of convenience such common constructs or shared constructs may have, in other words: how far-reaching experienced commonality may be. Do I feel and act, do I construe more 'as a German', 'as a West German', 'as a West German on the left edge of the political scope', 'as a psychologist', 'as someone of the generation born in the war, now in his Fifties'?

Back to history:

In 1989, with the economic situation in East Germany continuously worsening, and more and more people illegally leaving the country through Hungary, Czechoslovakia and Poland, the revolutionaries did not primarily aim at unification. The slogan of the mass demonstrations would be: '*We* are the people' as opposed to the government pretending to speak for the people. Gradually over the months in 1989, this changed to 'We are *one* people', thus indicating a wish to unite with the West.

Following the first democratic elections in East Germany, a fatal decision was made. The West German constitution allowed for two possibilities of uniting the two Germanys: the East simply joining the West, or two states negotiating a federation with possible changes on both sides. The choice was in favour of the former, which meant also the implementation of West German ways in nearly every aspect of everyday life in the East, including names of offices, streets, shape of forms, traffic regulations etc. So the necessary set of everyday anticipations was shaken to the ground, and is still being invalidated continuously.

Of course, the other side was the economic side: the breakdown of the East German industry which had lost its Eastern European markets and could not compete with the West German industry because of low productivity, lack of market access and obsolete administrative structures.

So one pole of the old construct according to Kelly's observations: Social security, was shattered. But one construct still holds: West Germans are construed by many East Germans as *over-competitive, individualistic, egoist*, members of a so-called *elbow society* as opposed to East Germans as being *poor* but *modest, people-orientated, neighbourhood based caring* persons. So after a time of transition with more symbiotic constructs, like 'one people', an old construct seems to be revived.

West Germans appear to construe themselves as *hard-working, justly prospering* people and the East Germans as *lazy, authority-dependent, always complaining weaklings*.

Since these constructs don't match, misunderstanding is frequent. Sociality in Kelly's sense is not well developed. Remember the slogan I quoted with the East Germans hollering 'We are one people' at their government: Now there's a joke often told these days: A West German ('Wessi') and an East German ('Ossi', a term derived from Ost-Deutschland) meet. Says the Wessi: "We are one people". Says the East German: "We too".

So I would like to pose some questions or issues to think about:
- How much of German group reality is a common reality because of the national history from 1871 to 1945 (because Germany as a state was established only in 1871)?

- How much was established during the 45 years after WW II?
- How much in personal construct systems (e. g. mine) is contributed to by the different group and group realities which I am part of and to which I contribute myself?
- How much of the difference in East and West German group realities is due to simple economic facts like an unemployment rate of 16% in East and 7% in West Germany? What does that mean for anticipating the personal future?

I think we ought to know much more about the construction of group realities than we do now. The chapters in a book of that name (Kalekin-Fishman & Walker, 1996) provide some guidance.

Being part of this process, I am looking forward to the future development - and how it will fit into the larger scale process of constructing *European* group realities.

References

Kalekin-Fishman, D., Walker, B. (Eds.) (1996). *The construction of group realities.* Malabar/Florida: Krieger.

Kelly, G.A. (1962): Europe´s Matrix of Decision. In: Jones, M.R. (Ed.): *Nebraska Symposion on Motivation.* pp. 83-123. Lincoln, Nebraska: University of Nebraska Press. (*reprinted in this volume, p. 12-44*).

GOING PLACES

Travelling: 'We don't call it travelling; we call it living'[16]

Beverly M. Walker

Why do a paper on travelling?

1. It forms an increasingly important part of people's lives and there are no psychological theories about it, nor is it integrated into the existing theories.

2. Many travel writers seem to be quite explicitly personal construct advocates in that they frequently write in terms of contrasts. 'This hotel is for the family-oriented, rather than the single seeking excitement', etc. Also they often make statements that bear considerable similarity to what Kelly says about encouraging venturing, exploring, adventuring. Kelly of course wrote about his own travel, but focused more on the experience of others, not on that of himself or his wife.

> *The person who attends only to what is familiar is not likely to become psychologically mature, nor can it be said that his life experience is enriched* (Kelly, 1959, p. 24).

> *Travel broadens the mind*

3. It is in the extraordinary moments that we see what is going on (Kelly, 1977; Mair, 1989).

4. Perhaps because of this in travel the processes of our construing are more obvious than in our everyday living. The events that lie outside of our construing system's range of convenience are more discrete, distinct. In particular it is changes in construing that become more explicit. Yes, but you might say that that is so in therapy also. It is, but I suspect that, since some of the change occurring when we travel concern less core construing, it is easier to see what is happening. At any rate it may be easier for us to reflect on our own construing when we travel than when we are engaged in the emotion-laden process of therapy.

Not that travel is not emotion-laden, but in many cases it is tolerable, partly because we frequently know when it will end. Many travellers find that it is relatively easy to time- or space-bind the experiences.

---

[16] Reprinted from Scheer, J. W. (Ed.) (2000): *The person in society – Challenges to a constructivist theory.* Giessen: Psychosozial-Verlag (16-28).

The travails of travel

It is interesting to note the etymology of the word 'travel'. It was once the same as 'travail', meaning bodily or mental labour, especially of a painful or oppressive nature; exertion; trouble; hardship; suffering.

When we travel it is often hard work.

We are constantly faced with puzzles that we cannot solve. They may be simple. In Australia we walk on the same side of the pavement, stand on the same side of the escalator, as we drive on the street. Logical, isn't it! In the UK you don't. You stand on the escalator on the opposite side. So Australians continually find themselves inadvertently in the wrong place in the middle of the rush hour, being mown down by hurtling commuters.

The simplest, apparently everyday things become an effort. Our predictions of the most mundane things are awry. We all know the hazards of crossing a road when the traffic travels on the 'wrong' side. At the Barcelona Personal Construct Psychology (PCP) conference the hotel reception staff decided I was most peculiar. After I got settled in I did a quick check round my room and was unable to find an iron. Now in Australia not every hotel room does have an iron, but many do. The iron-less rooms are usually in hotels that provide laundry facilities on each floor, or perhaps centrally, or else you borrow an iron from the front desk. So down I went to the desk, and with copious gestures eventually communicated, after about 10 minutes of non-comprehension and various staff being brought in to interpret, what I wanted. No, they indicated, no irons. Hotels in Spain do not have irons available for guests. If you want to smooth the creases from the trip you pay to have your clothes laundered.

Such problems pale into insignificance however in comparison to those one experiences in India where, for example it took my friend and myself five days of constant all-day-every-day effort to get train tickets out of Delhi.

How do we feel?

Some measure of anxiety is seen as a correlate of adventure. (Kelly, 1955, p. 1111)

When we travel most of us experience overwhelmingly anxiety. We continually live with the experience of not understanding what exactly is happening around us, not knowing what to do in order to achieve what we accomplished effortlessly at home. This is exacerbated if we do not speak the language and is far worse if we cannot read the script. For example colleagues were visiting Israel and while staying at this kibbutz decided to go down to the beach for a swim. They were directed down a dirt track and eventually reached a gate with a large notice in Hebrew on it. They were full of trepidation. What did it say? 'Beach this way' or 'Keep out. Land mines ahead' or 'Army property'. Needless to say they didn't have a swim that day.

At times our experiences are threaded with fear or even threat as constructs concerning one's very identity are under challenge when we are confronted with contrary or non-validating evidence. Indeed this challenge to identity is an end which, in some contexts, has been the basis on which young adults have been encouraged to undertake the 'Grand Tour' of Europe as a necessary prelude to the achievement of maturity.

To minimise the anxiety, fear and threat people can adopt various strategies. One is to read as much as possible about the place before they go to increase the degree of predictability. Another is to go on an arranged tour or with a well-travelled, well-organised companion who preferably speaks the language, so someone else deals with the unpredictabilities. We stay in good hotels when in places that are most likely to assault the senses, dilate our systems. These could be seen as examples of controlled elaboration.

Sometimes it seems that the camera or video recorder also serves the purpose of reducing our anxieties, making these pieces of equipment into what Winkler (1997) called 'security blankets for grown-ups'. We deal with our alien surrounds at one remove, through a lens. The challenge is framed, focused, confined, so that 'strict borders and boundaries (are placed) on an otherwise limitless experience' (Winkler, 1997). Much of it we may not really see until we bring it home and watch it in the security of our own living rooms. As we provide a commentary to our video on our travels we are making a link to home, one which removes us somewhat from what we are videoing. The photographs we take are for others, or for the self which we are at home.

So there are many negative consequences of travel which raises the question of what we get out of it.

Why then do we travel?

In this section I am going to discuss some of the positive consequences of travelling. Some of these may provide the motivation for us to travel in the first place, but others may be unintended by-products initially, outcomes that may lead some people to become inveterate travellers.

A freedom from everyday obligations and responsibilities would seem to be a common reaction to travel. I am always struck when I get on the plane for the long flight to Europe or America how quickly I feel release. It's always a tremendous effort to get ready, with papers to prepare, courses to process, my family, pets, and research students to get organised, as well as the myriad details of the trip itself. I get on the plane exhausted, usually with some things not completed. But seemingly, as soon as the plane levels off, these responsibilities, so absolutely critical while at home, pale into the background. It doesn't matter. They're not important. The superordinates have changed - though crucially it's mostly a temporary re-arrangement. We are having a holiday not only from our everyday surroundings and responsibilities, but from some of our core and superordinate constructs, or at least how they are applied.

There is a freedom too in not having a pre-conceived construction placed upon you by others you meet. When living in London in the 1970's I seemed to be surrounded by Antipodeans who had slot-rattled in the absence of the constraints of family expectations. They knew however, that this was a temporary change. They would return home and most commonly resume their more conservative persona. There are, however, the stereotypes that people have of you because of your nationality, but people will often tolerate your eccentricities – because you are a foreigner.

Travel is a kind of delinquency, more often rooted in the compulsion to escape the boredom and responsibilities of home than it is in any very serious desire to scale the Great Pyramid of Cheops or walk the length of the Great Wall of China (Raban, 1994, p. 15).

This quote in which travelling is viewed as 'a kind of delinquency' suggests that by travelling we can explore re-construal, particularly of self, in ways that are relatively free of the constraints of home. Here we see a major difference with therapy re-construal. It is probably a lot easier if we explore different ways of being when crucial others are not immediately required to re-construe as well, or if they are, we are not in their immediate vicinity to experience the full force of their struggle and resistance to such change, with its attendant invalidation.

Of course ultimately, if we decide we like the outcome of our experimentation, on our return home we still must deal with the 'communal inertia or even resistance to change' (Stevens, 1997, personal communication). But by then validation has strengthened us, the fragmentation within our system has been reduced and we are more able to fight for our re-construed perspective; we may have developed re-construals that transcend the conflict, so that we may, for example, no longer see our family as so important to our lives, and they may also have re-construed our relative roles as well as their own identities.

Travel is in a very real sense an aggressive activity; we are actively extending our construing system, or at least some of us regard it in that way.

I travel not to go anywhere, but to go. I travel for travel's sake. The great affair is to move. (Stevenson, 1994)

One does not travel, any more than one falls in love, to collect material. It is simply part of one's life. (Waugh, 1995).

Our nature lies in movement; complete calm is death. (Pascal, 1961).

Travel...entails free fall in foreign space with only the slimmest of lifelines tethering the traveller to his home. It's an act of optimism, a hunger that no number of wonders can appease. A disease, for which the symptoms are many. (Oakley, 1993).

The good traveller is an inveterate snoop, always ready to poke his nose into other people's business and ask impertinent questions....you have to ask some odd questions when you're trying out someone else's life for size....it's a risky exercise (Raban, 1994, p. 18).

But for some, of course, the strategy used to cope with the new stimulation is hostility. Wherever they are, whatever the customs or scenery or politics, the hostile decry the different, the new, reacting to those around them in ways which are rude and inconsiderate. Nothing is as good as what they get at home. And, if people don't understand what they say, they talk louder.

Donald Horne contrasts those who go to see places and those who go to 'do' them. He develops this distinction in a delightful, if somewhat elitist fashion, by advocating a suggestion made at a 'Save Venice' conference that a Disney-like essence-of-Venice be constructed on the Italian mainland so that tourists could 'do' it in an hour or so, without contributing to the destruction of the real thing. Many travel writers have used the term 'traveller' vs. 'tourist' in ways that correspond with Horne's distinction. For himself he contrasts 'sightseeing' and 'sight-experiencing'. The former "can just mean looking without seeing" whereas with experiencing "you have a sense of its past and how it is now being used. You get something of your own out of it" (p.15).

I dislike feeling at home when I am abroad - George Bernard Shaw

Validation and invalidation

Shaw is perhaps extreme in this respect. For most of us it is important when we are travelling to have at least something with us of home. We need reminders that there are areas we can predict, that the ease and regularities of at least some of the details of our lives are maintained. E.g., at one time I was showing two prominent PCP visitors around the beauties of the Illawarra. We'd been to Bushranger Bay and were on our way to drive up Macquarie Pass to see something of the highlands. The American visitor pointed out a

McDonald's restaurant. I assumed that this meant he was hungry and said we'll stop at the top of the pass where there is a well-known pie shop. But when we got to the pie shop it turned out he wasn't hungry at all. What he had wanted to do was go to McDonald's. He then came out with a quote I've been dying to use in a paper - 'McDonald's is the closest thing to an absolute truth that I know'.

Sometimes it is important parts of our very identity that we need to be reminded of. We wear tee-shirts or other clothing that assertively proclaim our origins. We take pictures of family members and place them prominently around our rooms or in our wallets. We find ourselves conversing actively, sometimes desperately, with fellow country people whom we would have little (apparently) in common with at home. One of the PCP group in Wollongong described how, when living in Greece, she would follow tourists around the streets just listening to them speaking English.

When we travel with a partner or friend we have an accompanying validator of our construing, particularly our construing of self. This provides our experiments with a protection that they wouldn't otherwise have. We also have an ally who will often have the same problems with the same things as we do. But that comes at a cost.

Travelling in pairs and families is the continuation of staying home by other means. (Raban, 1994, p. 16).

Loneliness makes things happen (Raban, 1994, p. 18).

We start risking things that we would never risk at home. 'This is how adventures begin. This is why people find themselves waking up in strange beds and don't go home again. (Raban, 1994, p. 18).

When we travel on our own some of our crucial testing involves construing that may be quite core, concerning our dependencies both on self and others. We may be forced into a pattern of depending that is very different from our customary ways. In order to assuage our loneliness and aloneness we engage with others more readily, initiating interactions in ways that are contrary to our home-based reticence.

It was where I first felt I was an individual, on a journey (Cook, 1993).

Often when we travel we are seeking to validate things - seeing whether London or New York is as exciting as it seems in books or on TV. Travelling, however, is also inviting invalidation.

The traveller as experimenter

Previously I have pointed out that the model of the scientist was for Kelly the ideal of how people should be, rather than a description of how they currently operate (Walker, 1992). That is Kelly (1955) saw people as 'incipient scientists' (p. 13), not always as effective scientists. Considering the traveller as scientist we can further clarify the role of this model. What he advocated was that people *should* test out their hypotheses, conduct experiments, and take account of outcome to revise their construing in the light of the evidence in order to improve the predictive utility of their system. But not everyone uses this process as an ideal scientist does. Sometimes they avoid testing out their hypotheses, don't experiment, cook the books with regard to the evaluation of outcome, ignore evidence contrary to their hypotheses etc. This is what we call nonvalidation (see Walker, Oades, Caputi, Stevens & Crittenden, 2000). People adopting nonvalidation strategies abdicate their potential as scientists. While all of us are capable of performing all the stages of ideal science, we don't always do that, certainly not all of the time. However for Kelly our progress, our moves towards construing reality more clearly and veridically, depend on us completing the cycles of our experimentation.

When we travel we are confronted with both new experiments, as we struggle to make sense of experiences that are novel, and old experiments where the outcome is often different from what it had previously been. When we travel our scientist-like features can be working overtime. To begin with we are confronted with many new events to be construed.

Changing construing

> *To make sense out of concrete events we thread them through with constructs, and to make sense out of the constructs we must point them at events.* (Kelly, 1955, p. 122)

Changes in events, changes in elements, are of relevance to changed construing, and it is precisely the addition of new elements that travel centrally entails. We see previously unseen things, we feel new temperatures, textures, shapes, we observe other people's lives and puzzle at their customs, we taste different foods, smell unusual smells, listen to unheard sounds. In fact we can feel bombarded by these new elements, as people often report who travel to India or through Asia. Our construing system rapidly dilates.

> *One cannot make changes in an event column without making at least minimal changes in a construct row.* (Kelly, 1959, p. 22)

So what happens in such situations? How does our construing systems react? (Let's leave aside for the moment the situations where it doesn't cope well.)

In some cases the range of convenience of our existing construing systems expand to encompass the new experience. eg. these Buddhist temples are really another version of our Christian churches. We interpret the new element as similar to what we had previously known, subsuming it within a pole of a construct. But is the construct then the same as before? Presumably not, though the change to the system is minimal. We have reconstrued from within the existing system (Stevens, 1997).

At other times the new element(s) or the confrontation with a different hierarchy bring(s) about a re-arrangement of the hierarchy. Things change in their importance, given the incongruence. In India one is often confronted with situations which de-emphasise the importance of individuals' lives. eg. when I was in Delhi the fact that a building had collapsed killing 80 people made p. 3 of the newspaper, a small item of a couple of inches column space. Although this situation didn't lead me to change substantially my own hierarchy, for others the experience of India, the understanding of reincarnation, the experience of the sheer density of population, has led to substantial changes in what is considered important.

> *By judiciously introducing new elements into the client's field of experience, the therapist may so change the content of the construct contexts that the axes of the client's system are rotated. The same words may be used to symbolise the constructs, but the meanings may have been subtly changed* (Kelly, 1955, p. 939).

These changes are occurring at a time when the validation process might not be working very effectively. The testing out of our construing crucially depends on the reactions of others (Walker, 1990). When we are travelling on our own, and/or have little contact with locals and/or are in countries where we don't speak the language, we are deprived of the effective validation network that we have available at home. Sometimes too we put the testing out phase on hold, until we return home. Perhaps we act on the hypotheses in a way that holds them tentatively, as space- or time-bound, to be reviewed down the track in a different place, at a different time. They may be regarded as relatively incidental constructs whose relevance to more concerns may be explored at a later point.

Conflicts between construing of different groups may manifest itself when different construing, often for the first time, leads to clashes. At the Seattle PCP congress the biggest source of conflict was not whether we should redefine ourselves as constructivists or not, not whether construing is personal or social, not even where the next conference is to be held nor the perennial question of whether or not we should form an international grouping. No. The biggest conflict occurred over *the meaning of dinner*. When I reflected on it I realised that this was not a new conflict. It had been around in the theory group for some time, presumably since we started holding international congresses.

The first inkling of a problem came when we read the programme and found that some sessions had been scheduled for after dinner. There was a one hour dinner break. But there were those who regarded dinner as a leisurely activity to be undertaken with friends whom we may not have seen for a couple of years, savoured and planned to allow the maximum informal time for those valuable conversations that often are the most productive work-wise, as well as being socially and gastronomically rewarding. There wasn't time to dine. We voted with our feet, missing out on something that, at some other time, we would have chosen to attend. From the organisers' perspective it seemed that they had attempted to fit a very rich program into limited time and hence were concerned not to waste it. Further, I assume too they were understandably interested in providing activities for newcomers, who might not readily find themselves in a dinner group. Our non-attendance quite naturally upset the organisers, who were extremely hospitable, responsive to our needs, and concerned to make every detail of our stay as enjoyable as they could manage. Their solution was to 'send out for pizza'!

Nor were the restaurants always conducive to our concept of leisurely dining. In a culture where the take-home pay of those serving is largely dependent on tips, rather than wages, the more people in and out of the door, the greater one's pay. Eating is overwhelmingly done efficiently and quickly, to fill one's stomach, and then it is on to the next thing. Fast food is indeed the name of the game.

The outcome of this clash of meanings was not clear, but for some us at least it led to an increased understanding of something we'd not previously thought much about, something we had taken for granted given the similarities of the construal of dinner within a culture.

Travelling and changes of construing

The conditions of travelling correspond very closely to those that Kelly felt were instrumental in fostering change. In discussing therapy Kelly outlines conditions of favourability for changes in construing. The first of these was *use of fresh elements.* Travel is to a large extent undertaken precisely for the purpose of being exposed to new elements.

> *The elements, being relatively unbound by old constructs which would be seen as being incompatible with the new construct, do not involve the person with the old constructs until he has brought the new into a state of usefulness.* (Kelly, 1955, p.161)

"New constructs", he suggested, can be applied "with less danger of para-lysing effects" (Kelly, 1955, p. 161) if in situations where family members are not around. He writes of two further conditions. The first is *an atmos-phere of experimentation*, so that constructs can be tried out in relative isola-tion from each other ("the atmosphere of experimentation is one in which the consequences of one's experimental acts are seen as limited. One does not 'play for keeps'"; Kelly, 1955, p. 162-3). Thus our trip can be seen as a labo-ratory, relatively insulated from the rest of our lives.

> *A laboratory also provides a convenient insulation from other vari-ables, the complexities of which might swamp the person who is trying to form new constructs in a necessarily limited sphere. If one consid-ers at once all the ramifications and ultimate consequences of each exploratory act, he will be overwhelmed and unable to formulate any new constructs.* (Kelly, 1955, p.169)

The last is *availability of validating data*, which has been discussed previ-ously.

Thus the process of travelling places us in situations that are highly condu-cive to changes in our construing system. Elements, and particularly new elements, have not been given their justifiable importance within personal construct theory. It is perhaps largely with respect to the availability and adequacy of validating data that travel most departs from therapy in not en-couraging constructive revision.

Returning home

Much of what is crucial about the effects of travelling only comes to pass on our return home. Some people come home and resume the life they had left off, with little change. In some cases this may have been a slot rattle. But for many, perhaps most, there are some more fundamental changes, many of them totally unexpected. Exploring this phenomenon tells us more about how construing changes.

After I returned home from six months living mainly in London I was driven home from the airport and couldn't take my eyes off the sky. I felt I had never seen sky before. The sky was clear blue and stretched forever. I had spent my time abroad in the narrow streets of London, with the buildings rising up on either side of the street to interfere with the expanses of sky, which irrespective had been cloaked in grey clouds for months at a time. In case you think this a peculiar idiosyncratic response, another friend several years later had a similar experience. So amazed was she to see the clear, blue sky of home that she lay down on the ground and took a picture of it.

Here in this room are many things which we cannot perceive. Some of these lie outside the range of our perceptual equipment. Others are present without their contrast so to us they are imperceptible. (Rowe, 1996)

Well what is happening here? What does this tell us about construing? The sky of home was not a new element; I had grown up with it. But presumably I had not had anything to contrast it with. It is not that the skies of home are always clear and blue. Perhaps I had distinguished overcast from clear skies, but because the latter predominated this was not a particularly important construct. Now I had a very elaborated contrast.

But there was more. Each pole took on additional meaning, importantly of a bodily nature. As I stared at the infinity of sky I soared. My body felt free, unfettered, no longer confined by the predominant melancholic greyness and constriction of body and movement that the European winter engendered. The element of sky stood for a construct of multi-layers and considerable complexity. This was what Kelly (1955) termed a symbol. But this phenomenon of seeing something familiar for the first time is very instructive.

For many the return home results in a consolidation of identity. Frequently this entails coming home convinced that one's life is the best option available. But for others, particularly for those who have been away some time, things can never be the same.

Conclusion

Travel, it seems to me, plays an important part in our lives. Kelly encouraged us to venture forth, try new things, be new people, experiment with ways of seeing our worlds. Not all of us can do this all of the time, and Kelly was not advocating that. But some times, at some points in our lives, travelling may lay us open to re-construing, not just our environments, but ourselves.

The quote I have used in the title was a comment made by a caller on the 6th June, 1998 to the Australian radio programme 'Australia All Over', hosted by Ian McNamara. She and her husband were caravanning round Australia following her remission from cancer. She said of their lifestyle – 'we don't call it travelling; we call it living.' Kelly made the comment: "When anxiety stifles adventure, then it is time to do something about it." (Kelly, 1955, p.1111). Maybe if more of us engaged in travelling, we would have less need to consult psychotherapists.

Acknowledgment

As with all papers it is important to acknowledge the input and support of the Wollongong Personal Construct Group. In this instance I am particularly indebted to Chris Stevens for elaborations of many of the ideas.

References

Cook, P. (1993). Interview broadcast on Australian Broadcasting Company radio, December 30th.

Horne, D. (1992). *The intelligent tourist*. McMahons Point, NSW: Margaret Gee.

Kelly, G.A. (1955). *The psychology of personal constructs*. N.Y.: Norton.

Kelly, G.A. (1959/1989). *The function of interpretation in psychotherapy.: Series of three lectures given to Los Angeles Society of Clinical Psychologists*, 1959. Wollongong: Personal Construct Group.

Kelly, G.A. (1963/1979). Psychotherapy and the nature of man. In B. Maher (Ed.): *Clinical Psychology and Personality: The selected papers of George Kelly*, 207-215. N.Y.: Krieger.

Kurasawa, S. (1994). The joy of travel. *The Australian Magazine*, Oct 15-16, p. 13.

Mair, M. (1989). *Between psychology and psychotherapy: A poetics of experience*. London: Routledge.

Oakley, B. (1993). That's that: nights errant. *The Australian Magazine*, June 12-13, p. 70

Pascal, B. (1961). *Les Pensées*. N.Y.: Dolphin.

Raban, J. (1994). Road to utopia. *The Australian Magazine*, Oct 15-16, 14-18.

Rowe, D. (1986). The importance of Personal Construct Theory. In B.M. Walker, J. Costigan, L.L. Viney, B Warren (Eds*.): Personal construct theory: a psychology for the future*. Melbourne: APS Imprint, 9-24.

Stevens, C. (1997). Personal communication, 27 May.

Stevenson, R.L. (1924). *An inland voyage: Travels with a donkey in the Cevennes*. London: Heinemann.

Waugh, E. (1995). *Ninety-two days: Journey in Guiana and Brazil, 1932*, Harmondsworth: Penguin.

Walker, B.M. (1990). Construing George Kelly's construing of the person-in-relation. *International Journal of Personal Construct Psychology*, 3, 41-50.

Walker, B.M. (1992). Values and Kelly's theory: Becoming a good scientist. *International Journal of Personal Construct Psychology*, 5, 259-269.

Walker, B.M., Oades, L.G., Caputi, P., Stevens, C.D. & Crittenden, N. (2000). Going beyond the scientist metaphor: From validation to experience cycles.. In J.W. Scheer (Ed). *The person in society: Challenges to a constructivist theory*. Giessen: Psychosozial-Verlag, pp. 100-113

Winkler, M. (1997). Travails in tourist class. *The Australian*, May 26, p. 15.

Identity and Travelling[17]

Beverly M. Walker

At the Berlin International Personal Construct conference, organised by Jörn Scheer, and held in Berlin I gave an invited address on aspects of the psychology of travelling (Walker, 2000[18]). Continuing with that theme, in this paper I want to take up a couple of issues concerning particularly identity and travelling. Specifically I will suggest that while much travel is an attempt to extend one's identity, broadening one's focus, there are some forms of travel that have the opposite aim, viz. the consolidation of existing identity.

For many of you, it will seem strange that a psychologist should be interested in travel. It is not a recognised area in psychology, though of course some have worked on issues concerning the marketing of tourist destinations (e.g. Pearce, 1991). Sociologists have had a greater interest (Urry, 2000). However, travel is an increasingly important part of people's lives, no longer an activity undertaken solely by the rich. In some cultures, it has been integrated into the normative expectations of individuals at particular times in the life-cycle. In Australia, the young often travel extensively overseas before settling down to family life. On retirement, the phenomenon of 'grey nomads' has become very prominent, with thousands of retirees slowly travelling round Australia in caravans and mobile homes.

It is particularly appropriate in a volume like this to write about travel. Jörn Scheer also has written an account that deals with some issues related to travel, particularly the problems of language across cultures (Scheer, 1996[19]). And most recently he has himself been travelling a great deal more, particularly to Australia. Hopefully at some point he might write more about this hands-on research into cross-cultural experience.

However one of the main reasons for looking at travelling is that it seems to me that the processes of everyday living become illuminated more clearly when we look at an event that is very different from our day to day living. It is striking too that many travel writers are natural personal construct theorists. They write about experience in terms of contrasts, what Kelly (1955) termed bipolar construing. They explore many experiences from the point of

---

[17] This paper was originally published in German as: Walker, B. (2001). Identität und Reisen. in: J. Scheer (Ed.) (2001). *Identität in der Gesellschaft*. Giessen: Psychosozial-Verlag (24-25).

[18] Reprinted in this volume, p. 70-81 *(Ed.)*

[19] Reprinted in this volume, p. 104-121 *(Ed.)*

view of the importance of venturing, stepping outside one's comfort zone, a view that Kelly also espoused. In my previous paper I explored the similarity between travel and psychotherapy from a personal construct perspective. This paper takes up further issues concerning changes in self and identity associated with travel.

The aims and consequences of travel

Travellers have a purpose in mind when they embark. Some do it for business reasons, but they are not the focus of this paper. Perhaps most people travel to enjoy themselves in some way by having a holiday. Holidays can be thought of as time out zones, where one is temporarily sealed off from most of the rest of one's life, from its problems, day to day stresses and patterns of interactions with familiar others. It is a carefree time. But commonly when one travels, particularly far from home, the experience can be hard work, fraught with anxiety and stress. Our sensory systems become overloaded with the differences around us, our problem solving capacities are tested to the full as we negotiate our day to day survival in places where the ground rules are unknown and unknowable. The simplest things become major hurdles to overcome. So the aim of the holiday and its effects may be quite different. We might aim to enjoy ourselves, but hard work and stress become the result – and the consequences quite unexpected.

The consequences of travel can have important implications from a psychological perspective. These can directly impact on the nature of the traveller's identity. While the *extension* of one's identity is often the consequence commented on and even aimed for, the kind of thing captured by the cliché 'travel broadens the mind', some travel has both as its aim and consequence almost the opposite effect. This kind of travel, pilgrimage, reinforces the person's existing identity.

Travel, identity and narrative

What I am suggesting here is that a useful way to think about travel is that it is an attempt to either extend or define our identities by entering into cultural stories that we are not currently centrally involved in. Travel for the extension of identity is exemplified by the Grand Tour.

Travel as an extension of identity

The earliest traceable reference to the 'Grand Tour' was by Richard Lassels in 1679 in *An Italian Journey, or a Compleat Journey through Italy* (Trease, 1967), though the benefits of travel had been commented on by prominent writers. For example, Francis Bacon (1625/1860) writes of the consequences of travel.

> ....let him not leave the countries where he hath travelled altogether behind him; ...And let his travel appear rather in his discourse than in his apparel or gesture;...and let it appear that he doth not change his country manners for those of foreign parts: but only prick in some flowers of that he hath learned abroad into the customs of his own country (p. 139-140).

The Grand Tour became very popular in the eighteenth century among the wealthy classes in Britain particularly (Black, 1985). Young men were encouraged to further their education by travelling in Europe to France, Germany and especially Italy. Accounts of the tour are varied in terms of their aims, value and benefits. Indeed, among the English some argued from a xenophobic stance that the tour was detrimental to English culture, bringing in extraneous foreign influences. For others this was its purpose, a broadening of cultural diversity within cultivated limits, achieved by changes in individuals with key roles to play in the cultural, intellectual and administrative future of the country. Its popularity among the British declined with improvements in transportation, particularly railways and the possibilities of mass travel that resulted in tours such as those organised by Thomas Cook (Trease, 1967). At the same time, it became more feasible for Americans and Australians.

> Through (them)... there is a sense in which the intrinsic tradition of the Grand Tour lives on, democratized and transformed on the surface, but in its impulses and aspirations much the same (Trease, 1967, p. 4).

Indeed a reverse phenomenon seems also to have been occurring more recently. Many young people from Europe venture to the so-called New World, America or Australia, to travel for extended periods of time, experiencing a sense of expanse, space and relationship to nature that is unknown within the confines of European living. What seems critical from a psychological point of view about this kind of travel is the focus on difference. People are seeking novel environments, and cultural experiences to widen their own experience of life. Such a contrast provides a point of comparison that has the potential to enrich one's sense of identity. Kelly (1955) writes about the importance of contrast, that we make sense of the world via bipolar constructs. Travel provides us with contrasts to much that is familiar, clarifying what our culture, and ourselves within that culture, is not. It also provides us with opportunities to elaborate our sense of self, as well as what self is not.

Travel as the consolidation of identity

This phenomenon of elaboration of self and cultural understanding was discussed more fully in Walker (2000). Now I want to turn to a form of travel, pilgrimage, that could almost be seen as the opposite in that it is characterised by an emphasis on similarity rather than difference. It involves the clarification and definition of one's existing sense of self as well as cultural positioning and understanding. I will focus on both religious as well as non-religious pilgrimage.

Examples of religious pilgrimage

The most common form of pilgrimage is that of a religious journey, whereby believers visit the sites allegedly associated with seminal religious events. Why do they do that? In some instances they attempt to gain in virtue in the sight of their god or gods, perhaps to accumulate brownie points to counterbalance their misdemeanours, to balance the ledger in their favour. At other times the aim is explicitly to obtain a greater positive - to have a miracle performed - to cure themselves of an infirmity, to make the lame walk, the dumb speak, the deaf hear, as many who visit Fatima attempt.

But frequently even religious pilgrimages have a broader aim, one most explicitly linked with identity. In undertaking a pilgrimage one attempts to place oneself within a broader story, to link oneself in a fundamental and inextricable way to a wider shared cultural narrative. One steps into the midst of what one has only been on the periphery of before.

Our peripheral status may be at odds with our core identities, as might be the case for many religious people. To see the sites/sights of Jerusalem and surrounding areas brings a reality to what has been read about in the Bible or the Koran. Thereby connection becomes more integrated, with the accounts fleshed out with more realistic visuals than the idealised and often conflicting ones that were part of religious education or cultural record. Now the visual is supplemented with our other senses - sounds, smells, bodily connections. The stories, so important, take on a more personally embodied form. We become centrally part of the narrative.

The extent to which people are prepared to go to extreme lengths to do this can be a wonder to others who do not share the link with the same cultural stories. Non-believers are amazed at the Islamic Hajj, where yearly people who have been included in their geographical allocation visit Mecca and perform a series of rituals with two million others, thus creating community among the faithful (Eichelman & Piscatori, 1990; Fernlea & Fernlea, 1997). By so doing they recall what is believed happened to Abraham and Isma'il when they made the Ka'ba into the sacred place of worship and peace. The cost of this pilgrimage is often great, with many saving throughout their lives to make the journey. Conditions in Mecca are frequently uncomfortable, very crowded and often dangerous, as the numbers who have died in the crush or fires attest. Nevertheless, pilgrims continue to visit, and return home to proclaim their new standing. In parts of India, such successful pilgrims have an elaborate picture painted over the mantel of their front door so others may recognise their changed identity.

These attempted connections to others past and present, this determination to link up with some broader story, may seem to non-believers somewhat ludicrous. As a person who was brought up in a Christian country as a Christian, I could understand something of those visiting Israel for a Christian pilgrimage, more so than those embarking on Jewish or Moslem journeys. The stories were at least familiar ones. However I looked on people's actions from the perspective of an ex-Christian and an atheist, fascinated by what I saw about other people's meanings. At the same time, I found much of it transparently unbelievable, and, as such, validation of my own meanings and identity. For example, at the Church of the Annunciation in Nazareth a very modern church had been built around a cave. This was the cave we were told where the angel came to tell Mary that she was to bear the child of god. The relevance of the cave had not been 'recognised' as such at the time, but several hundred years later it had been 'ascertained' to be this important site. The veracity of this designation was subsequently 'corroborated' by discovering a further hundreds of years later again a tunnel from the cave to a carpenter's shop up the hill a bit. That anyone would believe this literally seemed to me amazing.

The commercialization of people's identity changing journeys is often very blatant. The local kibbutz along the Jordan River made a bit of money on the side by baptising Americans. Something reminiscent of a sluice gate was set up in the river and lines of Americans dressed in white robes were waiting to be ceremonially immersed in the muddy water.

Despite how these sites appeared to a skeptic, those who believed appeared highly involved in the events that they were partaking in. It would appear that religious pilgrimages are not only conducted for extrinsic rewards such as merit in the eyes of God, but also for the more central defining of one's identity by linkage with others past and present, connecting with the elements of narrative shared and revered.

Example of non-religious pilgrimage

Not all pilgrimages are of a religious nature. Secular pilgrimages don't have the same obvious tangible reward value that many religious ones do. Their purpose is less clear to others but is tied up frequently in crucial issues of identity, particularly its greater definition.

To illustrate, Australians social commentators and historians have recently characterised the tourists visiting the Gallipoli peninsula and the battlefields of the First World War as pilgrims (McQuilton, 1999; Skates, 1998). April 25 has an important significance for both Australians and New Zealanders. It is a public holiday, generally marked by dawn services at cenotaphs and marches of returned service men and women throughout the country, as well as more recently their representatives. Its purpose is to remember the times of war and particularly those who lost their lives fighting for their country, though for some this memory is to reinforce the futility of war, whereas for others it is a celebration of bravery and nationalistic pride. It is called Anzac day[20].

The day itself marks what might be considered a peculiar event to commemorate - the disastrous landing of predominantly Australian and New Zealand forces at the command of the British, on the Gallipoli peninsula in Turkey in 1915. The place they were commanded to go ashore was the wrong place; the British command made a mistake. They should have landed south of what is now called Anzac cove. They were sent to a beach with a cliff above from which the Turks were able to shoot at will. The Anzac forces held out for many months, but the death count was about eight thousand. Eventually they retreated.

During the seventies, Anzac day was increasingly seen as an anachronism. But more recently there has been a steady growth in interest. Particularly since the seventy-fifth anniversary of the landing, Gallipoli itself has become a major focus. In 1998 more than 8,000 people attended the dawn service at Anzac Cove (McQuilton, 2000). What has been considered notable about the nature of this group is that it consists, not mostly of older people who have experienced war, but younger people who have not, young antipodean adults in their twenties back-packing around Europe. In Australia, this phenomenon has come under considerable scrutiny, though its understanding has not yet reached a satisfying conclusion. But those who have been observing it link it to issues concerning identity, and consider the age of the participants important to that interpretation.

There have been traditions of young adults in various parts of the world engaging in travel as part of the maturing process. In many countries, it is typically the case that university students go to university somewhere other than their home town. I have never heard a conclusive rationale for why this happens, but most commonly, it does in places such as the UK and US. While

---

[20] in honour of the *A*ustralia and *N*ew *Z*ealand *A*rmy *C*orps *(Ed.)*

historical precedents and geographical constraints are no doubt involved, presumably such cultures share the view that this is desirable for the bond between adolescent and parent to diminish, to allow the preparation for adulthood to be laid.

This pattern is not the case in Australia. Most adolescents go to university close to their home of origin, unless they are precluded from doing so by geographical or curriculum constraints. But the same necessity for separation between child and parent, the familiar and the unfamiliar, occurs. In this respect, an extended overseas trip is considered highly desirable, though its rationale has traditionally been in terms of the richness and superiority of (particularly) European cultural traditions and accomplishments. More recently, this cultural cringe has diminished and clearly the pilgrimage to Gallipoli is not part of this search for others' culture. Rather it would appear to be an assertion of Australians' own cultural place[21].

The Anzac legend has to do, in part, with the identity of Australians as distinct from the British, from whom white Australia, at any rate, in the early 1900's was centrally linked. Here at Gallipoli was played out the dilemma. Our roots supposedly were British, which was why the British officers were making the overall strategic plan, and hence the mistakes. At their direction the Anzacs fought, but it is the latter's valiant efforts, resourcefulness and self-less sacrifice, however misplaced in retrospect, that are commemorated. Here writ large is the necessity for our independence, as well as justification for it. There have been calls for the 25th April to become our national day, despite objections from feminists and anti-war protesters.

New Zealanders also have similar concerns. Their memorial is at Chunuk Bair, a ridge of which it has been commented: "How the New Zealanders took the position is almost impossible to understand. The seaward side of Chunuk Bair is almost a cliff" (McQuilton, 2000, p.7). But they did and held it for two days at enormous cost of life. However, they were relieved by the British, who lost the position, an important turning point in the failure of the Allies quest to reach the Dardanelles. 630 men lie in the Allies' cemetery there, with only 10 able to be identified. There remains considerable resentment by New Zealanders of the futility of the Kiwi sacrifice and resentment too that the Turks have erected there a giant statue to honour Atatürk, the man who drove the foreigners from Turkish soil (McQuilton, 2000).

So there is a sense in which, as Australians and New Zealanders, Gallipoli and the events that surround it provide a symbol of our difference from the cultural heritage we considered we had grown from. But for the young back-

---

[21] My understanding of the Anzac traditions is from an Australian perspective. Hence I will focus on what I know, though I assume that it is similar in New Zealand.

packers travelling the world there is further significance. At a time when their identity might be considered more fluid, engaged in an activity, travelling, that is conducive to loosening up one's constructions including one's constructions of one's self (Walker, 2000), participation in the events surrounding Gallipoli provides them with a touchstone, a more tangible definition of who they are and who they might be. It is perhaps not accidental that most of those travelling to Gallipoli for the ceremonies are of roughly the same age as those who were killed (McQuilton, personal communication).

I would like to suggest that such religious and secular pilgrimages can usefully be looked at as attempts to place oneself more centrally within a wider cultural story. We visit a place where others were centre stage, but it is others with whom we wish to better merge our identities, whether that identity be of religion or other aspects of culture. Thereby we attempt to define ourselves, as well as elaborate our understanding of our religion or culture. This is not simply a matter of increasing our understanding of important cultural events. As Donald Horne (1998) has indicated, "we don't have to 'do' the world to know it" (p. 12). Knowing isn't necessarily the issue. What *is* at issue concerns the definition of our identity to more centrally link with those who played out these epic events at that place. Thus, whereas it could be argued that travel by young adults is concerned with fostering their independence, in some cases at least it is their linkage with others that is the issue.

Similarity, contrast and identity

From a Personal Construct perspective, one can usefully think of these two consequences of travel, both the extension and consolidation of identity, in terms of Kelly's stress on the bipolarity of construing. By this he meant that we make sense of things by seeing some of them as similar and different from other things. Both the similarity and difference is critical, each being relative to the other, just as north makes sense only in relationship to south, or hot to cold.

Hence if we think of the construct 'self-not self', we can think of pilgrimages as attempts to elaborate the self-pole, to clarify and extend our existing identity. Our commitments and values are consolidated, rather than challenged. Who we are is massively validated by our sharing of what is important with others of similar persuasion. Change is not something we would expect to follow from such travel.

By contrast the form of travel typified by the Grand Tour can be thought of as an elaboration of the 'not self' pole predominantly, as individuals are confronted with the new and unknown. Of course, there may also be some elaboration of self involved resulting from the stresses and strains of travel, its demand on our problem solving skills, as well as the marshalling of different social supports. However, the emphasis in terms of the aims of travel is on the contrast pole. But this can bring about an explosive and unpredictable result.

In my previous travel paper, I wrote something of the consequences of on returning home. Many have written about the importance of culture shock and travel. Because travelling is frequently for a limited time we may bind our experiences to that time and space, placing spatial and temporal boundaries around the change, so that the effects while we travel are not so great. We try on temporary identities and see how they feel for a space and time that is delimited by what is on our itinerary. We have after all travelled precisely because we expected, even invited, new experiences.

But the biggest culture shock for many is to return home. Such change is not routinely anticipated, and even when it is, the disjunctions that confront us are frequently in areas we had not imagined. They sneak up on us when we least expect them. We see ourselves apart from something that previously we were enmeshed within, where we had been woven into the fabric so seamlessly that the threads were unnoticeable. The obviousness of life turns into questions, becomes something for which there are alternatives. We no longer see our surroundings as unproblematic, as inevitable, as what-is-and-always-should-be. The fabric can be woven in a different way.

In my earlier paper (Walker, 2000), I included an anecdote about my own return from Europe where I was unexpectedly confronted with the sky of home that I had never 'seen' previously. Something with which I had lived all my life I had never noticed before because I lacked something to contrast it with. I also had no reason to see any alternative. I used a quote from Rowe (1996), who is the only person I know to have written about this phenomenon:

> *Here in this room are many things which we cannot perceive. Some of these lie outside the range of our perceptual equipment. Others are present without their contrast so to us they are imperceptible* (Rowe, 1996, p. 13).

This relates to the issue that others have focused on, whether all construing is bipolar (Riemann, 1990; Millis & Neimeyer, 1990; Bell, 2000). We pointed out some time ago (Walker, Ramsey & Bell, 1988) that there is at least one form of construing, as set out by Kelly (1955), which is unipolar. That is preemptive construing, whereby things are seen as one thing only, the example given by Kelly being 'a ball is a ball and nothing but a ball'. Construing of this nature is very hard to work with, very hard to change. It's also not very useful as we cannot use it to make sense of new experiences. Much of the time we have experiences for which we have no contrast as the sky example illustrated. Having a contrast, recognising the contrast is an important facilitator of change and adaptation to new conditions. Bipolarity is perhaps better thought of as being desirable as far as composite sections of our construing system are concerned, rather than being of necessity the only way we can make sense of things. Such a view seems consistent with the empirical literature in this area, which seems to support much, but not all, of our construing being bipolar.

On our return from exploratory travelling however the seemingly familiar takes on a different colour, tone and feel. To paraphrase George Kelly, seeing the world through someone else's spectacles can permanently affect one's eyesight. We now have contrasts to things that were unnoticeable previously. Whereas we had only imagined one way to string together the pieces of a cultural necklace, other ways present themselves, and the importance of certain pieces is no longer unproblematic. This is not purely an intrapsychic process. It has important effects on those we interact with, those who may be forced to change themselves in order to accommodate the changes in us.

Not only is travelling hard work. It is also perilous. We don't know what will eventuate as a consequence. The normal processes of life are accelerated and magnified. Our very identity may be at issue. But many consider that the consequences have been worth it.

References

Bacon, F. (1625/1860). Of Travel. In J. Spedding, R.L. Ellis, D.D. Heath, *The works of Francis Bacon*. Vol 12, pp. 137-139.

Bell, R.C. (2000). A psychometric assessment of the bipolarity of constructs in Repertory Grid data. In J.W. Scheer (Ed.) *The person in society: Challenges to a constructivist theory*. Giessen: Psychosozial-Verlag, pp. 141-149.

Black, J. (1985). *The British and the Grand Tour*. London: Croom Helm.

Eichelman, D.F., Piscatori, J. (1990). *Muslim travellers: Pilgrimage, migration, and the religious imagination*. London: Routledge.

Fernlea, E.W., Fernlea, R.A. (1997). *The Arab world: Forty years of change*. N.Y.: Doubleday.

Horne, D. (1992). *The intelligent tourist*. McMahons Point, NSW: Margaret Gee Publishing.

Kelly, G. A. (1955). *The psychology of personal constructs*. N.Y.: Norton.

McQuilton, J. (2000). Commemoration and contested space: Gallipoli and 'ANZAC': A personal research note. Unpublished paper, University of Wollongong.

McQuilton, J. (2001). Personal communication.

Millis, K K, Neimeyer, R A. (1990). A test of the dichotomy corollary: Propositions versus constructs as basic cognitive units. *International Journal of Personal Construct Psychology*, 3, 167-181.

Pearce, P. (1991). Analysing tourist attractions. *Journal of Tourism Studies, 2*, http://www.jcu.edu.au/school/cea/tourism/vol2no1.html

Riemann, R. (1990). The bipolarity of personal constructs. *International Journal of Personal Construct Psychology , 3*, 149-165.

Rowe, D. (1986). The importance of personal construct theory. In B.M. Walker, J. Costigan, L.L.Viney, B. Warren (Eds.). *Personal construct theory: A psychology for the future*. Melbourne; Australian Psychological Society, 9-24.

Scheer, J.W. (1996). 'Congress language', personal constructs, and constructive internationalism. In B.M. Walker, J. Costigan, L.L.Viney, B. Warren (Eds.). *Personal construct theory: A psychology for the future*. Melbourne: Australian Psychological Society, 129-150. *(reprinted in this volume)*

Skates (1998). 'From a Brown Land Far Away': Australian Pilgrimages to the Great War Cemeteries, *Locality*, 9, 6-13.

Trease, G. (1967). *The Grand Tour*. London: Heinemann.

Urry, J. (2000). *Sociology Beyond Societies: Mobilities for the Twenty-First Century*. London and New York: Routledge.

Walker, B.M. (2000). Travelling: 'We don't call it travelling; we call it living'. In J.W. Scheer (Ed.). *The person in society: Challenges to a constructivist theory*. Giessen: Psychosozial-Verlag, pp. 16-28. *(reprinted in this volume)*

Walker, B.M., Ramsey, F.L., Bell, R.C. (1988). Dispersed and undispersed dependency. *International Journal of Personal Construct Psychology, 1*, 63-80.

Construing Berlin[22]

Jörn W. Scheer

The 13th International Congress on Personal Construct Psychology was held in Berlin (Germany) in 1999. This text was meant to introduce the participants to the city that hosted the meeting – by talking about ways of *'construing'* Berlin. But what does 'construing' actually mean when we are talking about a city? I think that 'construing' here means two things:

-   What does this city mean to me? How would I anticipate dealing and coping with this city?

-   What can I expect from the people living here, because they are likely to affect me most personally if I lived here?

Some 'facts' about Berlin

Of course, everybody knows something about Berlin, the biggest city in Germany, its capital, and the 'Divided City' for 44 years. Here are some of the 'facts' that *not* everybody will be familiar with.

Berlin became the capital of Germany only less then 130 years ago - till then, there was no state named Germany. What was known as Germany consisted of a number of kingdoms (among them Hanover, Bavaria, Württemberg, Prussia..), dukedoms, grand-duchies, principalities, arch-bishoprics and the like, and a couple of independent little republics like Hamburg or Frankfurt. Some of them had been incorporated into Prussia, though, during the preceding decades.

After the *war of 1870/71* against France, 'Germany' was united for the first time. Since Prussia was the leading power in the German coalition, its capital city Berlin became also the capital of Germany - and the symbol of Prussian-German militarism.

However, after the loss of WW I, it became also the capital of the first German Republic which was named after the place where the constitution was signed: the *Weimar Republic*. During the following 15 years Berlin witnessed the rise of the Nazi Party and then its 12 years' rule, and suffered near total destruction in WW II.

---

[22] Reprinted from Scheer, J. W. (Ed.) (2000): *The person in society – Challenges to a constructivist theory.* Giessen: Psychosozial-Verlag (44-53).

Now more than 50 years later, Berlin has become the capital again - taking over from Bonn.

What we call facts will certainly influence the construing process - but construing is more than acknowledging facts ...

How some 'Personal Constructivists' construe Berlin

To find out about what 'construing Berlin' actually means, it seemed natural to me to ask a couple of colleagues how they construe Berlin. And to find out about constructs - what do we normally do, as Personal Constructivists? We ask people to complete a Repertory Grid. And that's what I did. I decided to use as a context of convenience, a frame of reference, the cities where the last 5 International Congresses of Personal Construct Psychology had been held. So I asked a number of colleagues through email to complete a Repertory Grid with these cities as elements. Some answered, some did not, some apologised, some sent non-formatted comments, so now I am able to present the results derived from a small sample of 8 grids. The respondents come from three continents involved in PCP, and all of them are present here.

The elements

The elements were the following 6 cities: Assisi, Albany, Townsville, Barcelona, Seattle, and Berlin - 2 North American ones, 1 Australian and 3 European cities.

- *Assisi,* the city of St. Francis, situated high on a rock in central Italy, abounding with pilgrims, a city of the arts, founded in early Roman times with, today, just 25.000 inhabitants. The International PCP congress was held there in 1989, 10 years ago.

- *Albany* is the state capital of New York, a few miles up the Hudson River. Founded in 1614, it has 100.000 inhabitants and hosted the 1991 International PCP congress. *James Fenimore Cooper's* Leatherstocking is probably one of the best-remembered citizens from the times of the Boston Tea Party. And *James Mancuso* is probably the best-known citizen to the PCP community today.

- *Townsville* was unknown to me before I attended the 10th International PCP congress in 1993 although Captain James Cook spent some time there in the 17-seventies overhauling the "Indefatigable" behind the Great Barrier Reef. With about 105.000 citizens it equals Albany in size and is the largest city in sub-tropical Australia.

- *Barcelona* is home to one of the leading soccer clubs in Europe and the capital of the Spanish region of Catalonia. The 1995 International PCP congress was held in this 5 million metropolis on the shore of the Mediterranean Sea which dates back to the times of the Roman Empire.

- *Seattle* is not only the home of Bill Gates but also the rainfall capital of the United States, situated on the Northern Pacific Rim, and was the site of the last International PCP congress two years ago. It has somewhat more than half a million citizens and is comparatively young: some 150 years.

I asked the respondents to elicit 6 constructs from themselves using the triadic procedure and to rate the elements using a 6 point rating scale.

Three cases

The grids were analysed using the Calgary WebGrid Internet Grid Analysis Procedure which produces, among other results, two-dimensional Principal Components Graphs. Among the 8 grids analysed were

- two grids with a dominant first factor,
- three, maybe four clear-cut two-component structures, and
- two grids who follow what I think might be called a kind of circumplex model.

Fig. 1 shows a one-component structure with a clearly dichotomous main component: the *interesting, sophisticated, 'pacey'* European cities (which, however, *pose communication problems* to English language speakers) vs. *the uninteresting, unsophisticated, although laid-back* colonial places in both overseas worlds.

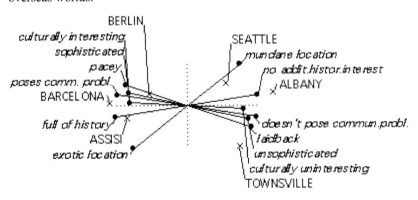

Fig.1: *A dichotomous construct system*

The two-component grids have in common that they accentuate a main component which is a bit similar to the above-mentioned ones, with a second component added that relates to different aspects of quality of life. The grid shown in Fig. 2 presents a Europe vs. USA dichotomy, contrasting *historic, interesting, exotic,* but potentially *dangerous* cities (Barcelona, Berlin) with *dull* and *young* cities (Albany, Seattle). The second component has a hedonistic touch to it, with *enjoying life, especially food*: Assisi (good) vs. Townsville (bad). The respondent added a commentary: "looks like I really liked Assisi. Well, I did"...

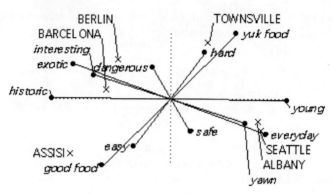

Fig. 2: *A two-component construct system*

The third group of grids have a less clear-cut structure: Fig. 3 shows a structure where the personal relevance of the places to the respondent seems important, and the places have distinctive features each: Assisi is *beautiful* and *safe*, Townsville is *difficult to get to*, the *dislike* of Albany is obvious, Barcelona is *easily reached* but *not safe*, and Seattle and Berlin are basically on the "good" side but not very distinct.

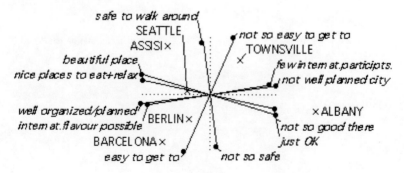

Fig. 3: *A circumplex type construct system*

96

Constructs about Berlin

A more detailed picture is derived from a content analysis of the constructs. 48 constructs were produced by the respondents. I have grouped them into two major categories: those who characterise the cities as such (Table 1), and those who describe their impact on the people (Table 2).

Tab. 1: *Constructs about Berlin – the city*

town with history **full of history**	no history no additional historical stories adding to interest
historic historical ancient medieval	young modern **modern** **urban**
centres of excellence **uniqueness** **interesting** **interesting** culturally interesting **richness** **romantic** **exotic**	day to day life sameness yawn dull culturally uninteresting emptiness routine everyday
world focus **more international flavour possible** **sophisticated** **suburban** **populated** **forward looking**	local focus not so many international participants would come unsophisticated rural isolation isolated conservative
scenic beauty beautiful place exotic location **green**	more mundane just OK mundane location brown
not commercial spiritual mystical	commercial materialistic **materialistic**

Both tables have a couple of subsections, and they show in **bold face** those constructs where respondents rated Berlin at the end of the scales, i. e. gave them 1 or 2, or 5 or 6. So from these two tables can be seen *how the respon-*

dents construe Berlin in the context of the other places that were hosts to PCP congresses.

Tab. 2: *Constructs about Berlin – meanings for the people*

laidback	**pacey**
relaxed pace	**hectic**
quiet + peaceful	**frantic**
still	**sensory overloading**
hot + slow	**energetic**
easy to get to	not so easy (to get to)
well organized + planned city	not as well planned city
easy (transportation/language)	hard (transportation/language)
doesn't pose communication problems	**poses communication problems**
nice to wander in	not nice to wander in
classy shopping	ordinary shopping
nice places to eat + relax at	not so good there
lots of small eating places	few small eating places
good food	yuk (food)
easy access to waterways	no access to waterways
devoted to tourism	not devoted to tourism
caters for tourists	ignores tourists
safe to walk around	not so safe
safe	dangerous
safe	threats of personal danger
hospitable	threatening

- We can see that Berlin is construed as a city *with a history,* yet *modern.*

- To the respondents, it is *interesting* and *exciting* (as opposed to *dull* and *boring*), and it is *worldly* and *sophisticated.*

- It is neither *beautiful* nor *ugly,* neither particularly *spiritual* nor *materialistic.*

- People here have to cope with *high-level tension* and *frantic activity.*

- It is considered a place for *classy shopping,* but apart from that, the *quality of life* is not particularly seductive.

- And *personal safety* does not seem to be an issue - this is probably due to the contrasting, rather unsettling Barcelona experience that some of the respondents may remember.

- To sum up, it seems that Berlin is construed as a true Old World Metropolitan City, exciting - but probably not your favourite retirement place.

Constructions of Berlin in Germany

Now let me say something about *constructions of Berlin in Germany* as I know them. One does not have to be a personal constructivist to notice the importance of dichotomies in describing the role of Berlin. First of all, everybody knows that for 44 years, Berlin has been 'The Divided City' par excellence, especially after the erection of The Wall in 1961. It fits with the impression that in construing Berlin, the German people are really divided (and this is not an East-West division). Perhaps it is also due to the multi-faceted history and the federal structure of Germany which lacks a dominant centre, as other countries have it in metropolitan cities such as London, Paris, Rome, Madrid, Athens, Budapest, Warsaw, Prague, Stockholm, Copenhagen, and all the others. Berlin was never the undisputed centre of Germany.

Interestingly, the division is so strong that in recent time the German parliament (as the prime authority in a modern democracy) three times has decided on matters relating to Berlin where normally a Government would decide. MPs were free to vote following their 'conscience' and not along party lines which is quite unusual.

1. The first one was whether Berlin was to become the capital city again after unification. That was always declared in the constitution but many people felt Bonn was a better place to have the Government than Berlin.

2. The second decision was about whether the world-renown 'wrapping' artist Christo should be allowed to 'wrap up' the old Berlin Parliament House (called *Reichstag*) which had been more or less a ruin since the disastrous fire of 1933.

3. The third decision was made only this year, and it was about a highly controversial Holocaust memorial to be erected on a huge area close to the Brandenburg Gate, in the heart of the city.

The first issue involves a most important dichotomy which is summarised in Table 3.

The people who preferred Bonn as the *de facto* capital construed Berlin as a symbol of traditional aggressive German chauvinism, with Bonn standing for a modern, post-war Germany with its close association with the West. The Berlin supporters pointed to the sophisticated metropolitan atmosphere and the symbolic opening-up towards the former Eastern block countries. As you may notice when you go downtown, the Berlin supporters won, although not overwhelmingly: the result is that the centre of Berlin is now the largest construction site in Europe, probably in the world, with Government and Parliament moving in these days.

Tab. 3: *Contrasts between Berlin and Bonn*

Berlin	Bonn
Northern (Eastern)	Southern (Western)
Prussian	'Rhine-ish': Bonn
Prussian	[Bavarian: Munich]
Protestant (Lutheran) or	Catholic
agnostic (East Germany)	Religious
upstart / parvenu / newly rich	ancient establishment
founded only 1244, big in 19th c.	founded 1st c. AD
rude / loud-mouthed	affable / soft
honest	false
big city (3.5 M)	small city (country) (290.000)
scary	comfortable
multi-cultural threat:	traditional safety / law and order
350.000 foreigners,	
'Turks & the Russian Mafia'	
Prussian militarism (WW I)	post-war Atlantic (West) integration
Nazi militarism (WW II)	European integration
sophisticated	provincial limitations
progressive / liberal	conservative
pulsating	sleepy
arts	small business
republican (Weimar, The Twenties)	outdated nobility

The second decision which was made a few years ago concerned the dignity of parliamentary institutions. Wrapping up the symbol of parliamentary democracy in silky material, to some seemed to mock the essential core of Western democracy. However, the majority considered *Christo's* and his wife *Jeanne Claude's* project as an outstanding example of modern, or rather post-modern artistic spirit and as such worthy of modern (or post-modern), art-loving, unpretentious Germany as we now like to be seen by the rest of the world. It probably helped that tourism benefited greatly from this event.

The third controversy which was finally solved through parliamentary vote concerned the size, the character, and the intentions connected to a memorial to the Jewish victims of the Holocaust. The area is still a huge wasteland close to the Brandenburg Gate. Discussions involving the Nazi Holocaust are still extremely intense, even tense in Germany; it can probably be no different even after more than half a century. But I am sure that the debates have been fuelled in part by the fact that the memorial site will be in Berlin, a few steps from the future seat of Government and of the Houses of Parliament, and will forever be a witness for 'the dark side' of modern Germany to every visitor and every citizen passing by.

About Berliners

All the things mentioned above are part of the national commonality in construing Berlin. Many Germans are scared by the big city as such, for while e. g. in Australia, the 'Outback country', 60 per cent of the people live in cities with more than a million residents, in Germany its only 8 per cent. Travellers fearing all kinds of metropolitan disasters may find their anticipations validated. On the other hand, you may be surprised to find subways pretty populated long after midnight, and they are normally considered reasonably safe - no comparison with New York or Barcelona...

Many German visitors expect Berliners to be rude and aggressive, and in fact they often seem to be. They think that themselves and take pride in having a 'Herz mit Schnauze', which means literally 'a heart with a snout' and signifies something like 'a loud-mouth with a heart of gold'. Knowing this, it is easier to construe this strange, almost proverbial rudeness as a defensive anticipation of an attack - and than to invalidate this anticipation by being relaxed and non-aggressive yourself. And personally I prefer the honesty and predictability of this behaviour to a certain non-committal niceness you may find elsewhere.

Of course, there has always existed a different construction of *'the Berliners'* during the last 50 years: occidental heroes surviving on an island in the Red Sea (remember John F. Kennedy's visit to the city), provided with the essentials from the outside through the airlift (as it really happened in 1948), separated from their brothers and sisters on the other side of the Wall - but then also the poor bastards we (the West Germans) had to feed and who wouldn't even say 'thank you'...

Moreover, for a long time, some quarters of Berlin were real refuges for all the hippies of the republic (after all, you couldn't be drafted in Berlin because it was not officially part of the Federal Republic but a four-power territory), then it became the largest Turkish city after Istanbul, Ankara and Izmir - and now they are getting uppity again, claiming their not-so-old right to be the leaders of the pack.

Back to the grids

Now after all this, what can we find in the grids completed by people who have seen the world but half of whom have never been to Berlin?

They do seem to capture some of the spirit that appeals to the outsider. However, looking at the constructs again, it is somewhat surprising that construing a city does not necessarily involve dealing with the people (or else in a threatening way). But then, it is probably different with me only because I happen to know Berlin and the Berliners (or some of them). For if I come to think of it, I have not met many residents in Assisi, or Albany, or Seattle myself. Maybe, an international conference is not the place to construe the locals - perhaps we should be content to construe Berlin as one of the centres of the post-modern world: Long live constructive internationalism!

SPEAKING IN TONGUES

'Congress language', personal constructs, and constructive internationalism[23]

Jörn W. Scheer

The initial story: Assisi

Meine Damen und Herren, während des Internationalen Kongresses zur Psychologie der Persönlichen Konstrukte in Assisi vor vier Jahren hörte ich einen sehr interessanten Vortrag über ‚Die Verwendung von Sprache: Eine konstruktivistische Sicht auf Politik und Moral'. Der Redner unterschied zunächst zwischen inhärenten und relationalen, also Beziehungsqualitäten. Die Zuschreibung inhärenter Qualitäten führt dazu, sich zu verhalten, als existierten diese Entitäten unabhängig von mir und meinen Konstruktionsprozessen. Alternativ dazu, so sagte er, können wir auch Qualitäten verwenden, welche Beziehungen zwischen Entitäten spezifizieren. Eine wichtige Art und Weise der Verwendung von Beziehungsqualitäten ist, äußere Ereignisse mit dem Sprecher in Verbindung zu bringen. Dies nannte er ‚Erfahrungssprache' und gab als Beispiel „Ich gebe mir große Mühe, Deinen Standpunkt zu verstehen". Er fuhr fort, indem er die Verwendung von Sprache der unterschiedlichen Arten mit politischen Aspekten der Ausübung von Macht und Kontrolle in Verbindung brachte. Etwas oder jemandem inhärente Qualitäten zuzuschreiben, bedeutet, eine Sprache der Machtausübung and der Kontrolle zu verwenden. Oft bedeutet dies, den Anspruch auf Besitz der absoluten Wahrheit zu erheben und die Wahrheiten anderer Leute zu negieren. Darüberhinaus beansprucht inhärente Sprache zu wissen, was real ist und, vor allem im Zusammenhang moralischen Urteilens, was gut und richtig ist und was schlecht und falsch. Erfahrungssprache läßt vielerlei permeable Realitäten zu. Wenn ich meine eigene Rolle in der Entstehung meiner Beziehungen zu anderen erkenne, sehe ich auch, daß der Prozeß wechselseitig kausal ist. Ich trage ebenso viel zur Erfahrung der Beziehung bei wie mein Partner. Wahrheiten werden relativ in bezug auf unsere jeweiligen Konstruktionen. Ich kann den Anspruch auf DIE WAHRHEIT nicht aufrechterhalten. Wenn ich eine Beziehungssprache benutze, betone ich Verbundenheit, Erfahrung,

---

[23] Reprinted from Walker, B. M., Costigan, J., Viney, L. L., Warren, B. (1996). *Personal Construct Theory – A Psychology for the Future.* APS Imprint. (129-149), by permission of the Australian Psychological Society. Copyright © 1996 The Australian Psychological Society Ltd.

*Gegenseitigkeit. Wenn ich mich für Beziehungsqualitäten und Erfahrungs-sprache entscheide, bin ich Teil der Vorgänge, denen ich begegne. Es wird einen fortgesetzten Austausch mit den Menschen geben, denen ich begegne, und mit meinem Gewissen, aber **ich** bin es, der sich dafür entscheidet, für meine Konstruktionen selbst verantwortlich zu sein, und für die Art und Wei-se, wie ich dieser Verantwortung gerecht werde.*

Ladies and gentlemen, friends and colleagues, after you have followed my speech for the last 2 minutes very patiently, I shall repeat what I have just said now in real congressual language. By this newly constructed term I mean nothing else but the good old English-American-Australian language. And from this enumeration you may see what I have in mind. For these three countries can be considered the Big Three as far as personal constructivism is concerned (to whom we might add Ireland as profiting from her colonial language). Is this due to pure chance? And also, is it pure chance that we have only a few threshold countries such as Italy. Spain, Germany, Norway, and the Netherlands with some PCP industrialisation, and a huge number of underdeveloped countries (see Figure 1)?

Fig 1: *A Personal Construct Psychology (PCP) map of the world*

Relational language

Now to the translation of my introductory remarks from my familiar German to the language most of you are familiar with!

*Ladies and Gentlemen! During the International Congress on personal con-struct psychology in Assisi 4 years ago, I was attracted by a very interesting title: 'Language use: A constructivist view of politics and morality'. The speaker began by making a distinction between inherent and relational qualities. The attribution of inherent qualities leads to acting as if these enti-ties are that way, independently of me and my construing. Alternatively he said, we may employ qualities that specify relationships between entities. An important way of using relational qualities is to link external events with the speaker This he rolled experiential language, and gave as an example: "I am struggling to understand your point": He then went on to link the use of lan-guage of different kinds to political aspects of exerting power and control. Attributing inherent qualities means using a language of power and control. Often, it means claiming to be in the possession of absolute truth and denying other people's truth. Moreover, inherent language articulates claims about what is real and, above all in the context of morality what is good and right, and what **is** bad and wrong. Experiential language, on the other hand, allows multiple permeable realities. As I recognise my own role in the generation of my relationships with other people, I come to see that the process is mutually causal. I contribute as much to the experience of the relationship as does my partner. Truths become relative to our respective constructions. I can no longer claim privileged access to The Truth. When using relational language, I emphasise connectedness, experience, and mutuality. Choosing to use rela-tional qualities and experiential language, I am part of the events I encoun-ter. There will be an ongoing negotiation with people I encounter and with my conscience, but it is I who chooses to be responsible for both my con-structions and how I exercise that responsibility.*

What I heard seemed to make sense to me. In fact, it conformed to some ideas I had already thought about myself. And yet, as I listened, I began to feel a bit uneasy. I was not sure if that was to be attributed to the concentra-tion that was necessary because of my limited knowledge of English. But when at one point the speaker said "as we change our language, our view of people is also open to change", I realised that in fact my uneasiness had to do with language problems. I took "change languages" in a more simple way to mean switching to a different (e.g., foreign) language, whereas the speaker meant something like "ways of using language". He used "I" and "we" fre-quently in his paper, but *my* positions struggling with language, trying to catch first the inherent meanings, possibly the relational qualities, then hope-fully what all that meant to me, was not part of his considerations. The speaker dealt with language, language use, and its impact on people and rela-tionships; it was an international congress he addressed, and he did not men-tion, probably did not even notice, that in the audience there might be listen-ers directly concerned by his theses.

The speaker finished. People began to discuss relational language in general and the consequences for psychotherapy in particular. I just sat there half-listening, remembering the one sentence about changing languages. Finally, I collected all my guts and made a few stumbling remarks in that direction, stating my opinion that unreflected use of elaborate English at an international conference raises the question of exertion of power, be the language inherent or relational, and asked whether such considerations would fit into what he had outlined. The discussants who followed me agreed with my point, and then there started a moving spiral of extremely relational language, in that everybody talked about himself. The English-speaking speakers accused themselves of English language imperialism, I protested that I didn't mean it that way, guilt feelings on the other side were expressed, I developed guilt feelings because I had caused guilt feelings, and so on. The final statement of one British participant was something like that, after conceding that there indeed is a problem, everybody would probably go on like he or she had done before. That closed the debate. And it proved to be prophetic.

And I decided - in secret, by myself - to write a little address to one of the following international congresses. I wasn't ready for that task in Albany. So, here it is.

And when listening, please keep in mind that, when I write a paper like this, I don't write it in German and translate it afterwards. I write it in English, because that is easier for me. To anticipate what I am going to explicate later: it is easier because I believe that thus I can come closer to English language constructs than when writing in German first. But it means also that, due to my limited knowledge and restricted, not to say constricted, vocabulary, the constructs I use depend on what I have learned during my English lessons in school, by listening to AFN (the American Forces Network) during my study years in Heidelberg, by listening to jazz tunes and pop songs, by reading novels and scientific publications, and what I picked up during holiday trips in English-speaking countries and, recently, at PCP conferences. These constructs therefore are *not* constructs that have been properly learned, and they are not constructs which have been developed by *living with the language.* They stem from something in between, with the shortcomings of such descent. And they have been validated only sporadically.

This may sound like an excuse. But in the context of today's topic I explicitly do not apologise for my poor English as I usually would. And I have refrained from having the manuscript corrected by a native speaker. What I would like to apologise for, however, is that I am going to touch upon a number of topics that transcend my professional competence. In some instances, therefore, what I have to say is more based on personal convictions or experience than on the solid ground of scientific knowledge.

One of the prerequisites of relational language is to make clear who you are when you are speaking; to stay or to become recognisable. And I may antici- pate, again, that this is a main feature of what I have understood of Miller Mair's (1989) concept of a *conversational psychology*. Therefore I shall make intensive use of relational language in the above-mentioned sense. That's why I want to say a few words about who I am. I was born in the north of Germany in the year when the German army invaded the Soviet Union. After studying some physics, I became a clinical psychologist and was raised postgradually in a department of psychosomatic medicine with a psychoana- lytic background. I teach medical psychology to undergraduate medical stu- dents, and my research interests during the last 25-odd years have centred around psychotherapy processes and psychological aspects of medical prac- tice. My first, then very superficial, acquaintance with PCP dates back to about 1964. My involvement became more intense during the 80s. I still do not consider myself a dyed-in-the-wool Kellian. But since I think that con- structivist ideas and especially personal construct theory and technique de- serve wider recognition, I have devoted some time and energy to spread The Word in psychology and medicine lately

Now I shall give you an outline of my paper: I have subdivided it into nine sections:

1. *The initial story about my experience in Assisi.* That's what you have just heard. I call that a story with Miller Mair's remarks about psychology as storytelling in mind. But more about that later.

2. *Relational language.* That was the essence of David Fisher's (1989) presentation in Assisi - for he was the speaker - which I have just tried to recall. I am convinced that this is a very important construct when you think about the discourse among scientists.

3. *Sociolinguistics and power.* This relates to Basil Bernstein's (1990) distinction of an elaborated and a restricted code of speaking.

4. *International relations.* With this, my special points of today begin: the role of language in international relations and in the relationships be- tween people speaking different languages on a smaller, person-to- person scale.

5. *Translations.* The fate of constructs, personal or general, when trans- posed by translations is considered here. Until now, the PCP movement has reached mainly English-speaking countries. I suppose that this has to do with some sort of language barrier which only very few can really cross.

6. *Short-story telling.* Miller Mair (1989b) has advocated considering psy-

chology as essentially being a discipline of storytelling. This makes the role of language a central one.

7. *Conversational psychology.* Another concept Miller Mair (1990) favours is to engage in developing a psychology based on discourse. I am very sympathetic to this idea, but again: conversations use language as the most important medium of communication, and therefore, language deserves special attention.

8. *Constructive internationalism.* What does all this mean for PC psychologists - not only when theorising on their own and applying rep grids to the subjects they deal with, but also when they try to take the general humanistic impulse inherent to the theory seriously, and engage in transnational, possibly transcultural conventions such as the International Congress on PCP?

9. *The concluding story.* My concluding story will be a historical one - a little scenario about what might have become of PCP, if once in history a different decision had been made.

Sociolinguistics and power

What David Fisher (1989) elaborated in his paper reminded me of the work of Basil Bernstein (1990). The psychologists among you will be familiar with Bernstein's distinction of two codes of speaking: the restricted code and the elaborated code. The restricted code is characterised by an insufficient, simplistic syntactic structure, often ignoring grammatical rules; using short, often incomplete sentences; using adjectives and adverbs rigidly; applying stereotyped phrases and formulas; and mixing facts and attributed causes. The elaborated code is made up of the opposite features. So, in fact, one could speak of two different languages.

According to Bernstein, the two codes can be assigned to two social classes, the lower and the middle class. And the mastery of one or the other of these codes is associated with social dominance. As you know, this issue has been discussed widely during the 70s, with respect to educational politics, and has done a lot to make people sensitive to more subtle means of exerting social power. It would be interesting to analyse links to the concept of inherent versus relational language.

What Bernstein has explored means distinctions within one language. But nowadays it is not rare that in one country you have two or more different languages, languages that are used by a relevant proportion of the population. Mostly, one language is prevailing. Speakers of other languages are kept restricted to a low social status - be they indigenous, aborigines, natives, or whatever you might call them, or immigrants of low social status, as long as they stay small in numbers.

Most of you will know what I mean because Americans, British people, and Australians have to face the problem likewise, as I am told. But also in my country we are familiar with it. We have about 8 per cent of foreigners who live permanently in the country, in cities like Frankfurt as much as 29 per cent. Many of them are so-called *guest workers (Gastarbeiter* in German) or *foreign co-citizens (ausländische Mitbürger)* to use an euphemistic or palliative term popular in public speeches and in the liberal mass media. They are Italians, Spanish, Portuguese, Greeks, former Yugoslavians, recently many refugees from Eastern Europe and the Third World, the largest group being the Turkish immigrants (or migrants because many of them do not consider themselves as immigrants although they in fact are). If they want to accomplish a rise in social status or be accepted in their neighbourhood, they have to adapt to the rules and habits of their host country. Sometimes, and especially in times of pressure and social upheaval, they cling together and it is their language which is used as the most effective medium for maintaining a national and cultural identity of their own, thus eventually hindering integration. This is not so much the case for the second generation, where children often act as interpreters or translators for their parents, thus reversing the common order of dominance or impact between the generations, but thinking in two languages certainly creates problems.

It follows from all this that language is an important tool in exerting social power. This is far from being a new insight, but has bearing for many seemingly small-scale occasions which are often overlooked.

International relations

In 1961 George Kelly and his wife travelled to 37 countries, many of them European countries. It was not a holiday trip, but a kind of field research. Some of the results were presented during the Nebraska Symposium on Motivation in 1962. The title of that paper was *Europe's Matrix of Decision* (Kelly, 1962[24]) and it was mainly about constructs that govern the position the inhabitants see for themselves and their countries in the world (especially the changing world, which was termed like that already then), and the constructs they use when viewing other countries.

Concerning Germany, he reported an observation on the change of image Germany had undergone by World War II. About Finnish people he said that:

like many other people they looked to *Germany as a fountainhead of*

---

[24] Reprinted in this volume, p. 12-44 *(Ed.)*

both science and literature. America, by contrast was the country where automobiles, aeroplanes, movie stars, illiterate millionaires, and addle-headed tourist came from. To a somewhat similar extent this axis of German scholarship versus American simple-minded materialism structured the thinking in other countries of Europe as well.

But there has been a curious shuffle since the war The same construct dimension still holds, but America and Germany have exchanged positions. Now it is the Germans who are the materialistic, money-conscious, crude-mannered vulgarians of the world, and it is the Americans who are exporting scholarship. (Kelly 1962, p. 115)

So much for Kelly after visiting Europe in 1961. It might be interesting to elicit constructs under the conditions of today's still more dramatically changed world, to include, for example, the then apparently not yet discernible role of Japan. Ironically, the cited view of Germany today is advanced by many East Germans looking at their Western fellow countrymen. The role of the United States within the context of scientific progress is still the same, and this has up to now a lot of consequences. English is not only the one 'congressual' language of the world; it is also the number one language for publications. English speakers or readers read or accept only what is published in English.

But the German scientists think the same way:

In our faculty of medicine presently the requirements for becoming a professor are discussed. One of the most important criteria is: how many publications have you published in an English language Journal? And they are weighted by the international (which means American) Scientific Citation Impact Index, which in our discipline looks like Table 1.

You can see that there is hardly a reputable journal published in German, and those listed have a ridiculously low impact factor. Now this may be all right in an American faculty. But we are in the heart of Germany.

But I think it is not the Americans who are to blame:

There goes a story that a high-ranking German NATO official (indeed a very high-ranking NATO official), when giving an interview to a group of German journalist (only Germans) insisted on giving the interview in English because English is the official language of the NATO.

I know a couple of colleagues who show slides and overhead transparencies with English texts to all-German audiences - thus implicitly indicating: "I have just returned from a very important conference abroad where I presented my paper very successfully, therefore I didn't care to produce a translated or re-translated German version of this slide for you" (but the chasm of ridiculousness has a narrow edge).

Tab. 1: *Science Citation Index: Impact Factors*

	Psychology			Psychiatry	
1.	Psychological Review	6.534	1.	Archives of General Psychiatry	7.918
23.	British Journal of Medical Psychology	0.595	43.	Nervenarzt	0.466
			45.	Fortschritte der Neurologie und Psychiatrie	0.431
28.	Zeitschrift für Psychosomatische Medizin und Medizinische Psychologie	0.345	48.	Zeitschrift für Psychosomatische Medizin und Medizinische Psychologie	0.345
			50.	Nervenheilkunde	0.193
31.	Annals of Medical Psychology	0.111	54.	Japanese Journal of Psychiatry and Neurology	0.100

The political dimension, and there we are amidst the international relationships, is of course important. It is a question of high importance to the governments involved, which ones are to be the official languages of the European Community: English and/or French and/or German and/or Irish, Italian, Dutch, Danish, Greek, Portuguese, Spanish, Letzeburgisch (which is the national language of Luxemburg along with the prevailing French) and more in the future? I really wonder how countries like Switzerland or Canada solve this problem in the long run without resorting to the Yugoslavian solution.

The times of - in chronological order - Kant, Hegel, Marx, Freud, Vaihinger, and Husserl are no longer there. And I might add: gone are the times of Voltaire, Montaigne, Galileo, Buddha, and Lao-Tse. And the role of their languages in the realm of science and philosophy is mere history.

Of course, this is not only the case with PCP, or with psychology in general; it is the same in almost every other field of science and civilisation. And the situation will probably remain like that also for the century to come. So there's no use crying about trifles.

Translations

When talking to people of other tongues, translation becomes crucial. What struck me about Kelly's report on his trip to so many countries was that he never mentioned language problems. From the fact that lie reported an interview with their Moscow interpreter about the decision why she became a psychologist (which was one of the topics the Kellys systematically explored in every country), one can deduct that they had local interpreters at hand whenever they moved to another country Since their main informants were psychologists and other intellectuals, it might be inferred that these people had at their disposal sufficient knowledge of English to discuss complicated matters with the visitors. It is left open to speculation what database could be collected this way, and what had to be left undetected.

When Ana Catina and myself prepared the edition of a two-volume introduction to PCP in German, we invited several friends from non-German speaking countries to participate in the project. In translating their contributions we faced some problems, part of them unexpected

Let me begin with the word *construing.* We have a German word, *konstruieren,* which belongs mainly to the technical world of designing an automobile, a house, or a computer chip. There exists also a figurative meaning which is used when you want to characterise, for example, the plot of a novel as unrealistic, artificial, far-fetched: it appears then *konstruiert.* Or if you see relations or connections between events or thoughts, they might be dismissed by a critic because they seem too *konstruiert.*

When consulting Webster's dictionary (1960, p. 177) I find that *to construe* means "to put into proper order by syntactical rules; to translate; to interpret". There is no equivalent meaning in German. Most people, however, who write about PCP in German use the word *konstruieren,* which makes the text difficult to understand for non-Kellians, and it sounds *konstruiert* in the above-mentioned sense of the word.

Similar problems arise when trying to translate terms such as *commonality.* Some people know what communality means when applying factor analysis. But my pocket Webster has only *commonalty,* meaning the common people, and *commonage,* the right of pasturing on common land - which may be of more importance in Australia today than in Old Germany.

When trying to translate *corollary,* I am first led into botany and then to something like *Hilfssatz* (helping sentence) or *Folgesatz* (following sentence), which nobody will understand. A last example is *grid.* My first acquaintance with the word was when I travelled in Scotland, and every two miles the unsealed roads were segmented by a *cattle grid.* I expect to meet more of them after this congress when I am going to visit the Outback. But how to translate the term? The English-German dictionary offers *Rost* (which means grid-iron, useful in barbecues) or *Netz* (which means a fisherman's net or has a figurative meaning like the railway system or the electric current distribution system) or *Gitter,* which means lattice or fence or railing, that is to say, some sort of enclosure.

In German, several of these words have been used. The translation of Bannister and Fransella's (1981) *Inquiring Man* (itself an untranslatable title) used the word *Netz* for grid (to me the least adequate solution). Other attempts include *Kelly-Gitter, Kelly-Grid, Konstrukt-Gitter, Kelly-Matrix.* The title we chose for our book is *Einführung in die Repertory Grid-Technik,* and we speak about *Grids* throughout (with the next question arising: does a Grid in German deserve a male or a neutral article?).

Now, I have to make clear that this problem arises not only within personal construct psychology. If you ever have a chance to read the German translation of the MMPI (with a knowledge of German as a background) you would alternatingly shake your head and chuckle. And after imagining how you would read this as a client, you would probably decide to abandon the test from your battery. And to translate Cattell's personality factors such as *Parmia*, *Premsia*, or *Praxernia*, would make a professional translator capitulate. Of course, this topic is not new. And the guild of translators around the world knows about that, probably since the days of Babylon. The art of translating novels and, still more hazardous, poems, has been subject to many thoroughgoing analyses. This is beyond the scope of my theme today, and I am a layman in this field anyway.

What I want to say is simply that the consequences of translating psychological terms are in my eyes insufficiently reflected. And this I consider astonishing with people concerned with meanings and especially with personal meanings. Because, comparing a German speaker and an English speaker with respect to personal meanings of a statement, a considerable amount will be accounted for by the variance 'between groups'. (It might be interesting to learn how many 'typical German' constructs, remaining hidden to me, you'll discover in my considerations.)

An amusing example is the translation of an English book: The spiritual heirs to Michael Balint (viz. Enid Balint and J. S. Norell, 1973, 1975) published a widely read introduction to patient-centred medicine under the title of 'Six Minutes/or the Patient'; alluding to the restricted time the general practitioner can afford to talk to the single patient, which however still enables him to have an eye on the doctor-patient relationship if he is appropriately trained. The German title is 'Fünf Minuten pro Patient': which means five minutes. Well, the translators did not mix up 5 with 6, and the German GP does not allot 20 per cent less time to his patient. It's simply that in Germany the

*decimal system has prevailed for more than 100 years (before that we had
dozens and miles and pounds, too), while at the time of the publication of the
book, in Britain it was still sixpence pieces you had jingling in your pocket.*

Now, applying these considerations to the PCP community, it is obvious that
mastery of the language also means mastery of the concepts and of the constructs. He/she who wants to be a member of the community should read
Kelly himself, which means Kelly in the original language: English. Without
that, graduation or initiation is out of sight. And so it is probably not by
chance that out of 124 articles published in the first five volumes of the *International Journal of Personal Construct Psychology,* only 16 have been
written by non-English speaking authors, and that most of them deal with
methodological aspects, not advancing the theory.

Why it is that some publications from the Italian group seem to contradict
this notion, I cannot explain.

Short-story telling

Miller Mair has written several interesting articles on psychology as storytelling, published in the *International Journal of Personal Construct Psychology* (1989b, 1990). Also in his beautiful book *Between Psychology and Psychotherapy: A Poetics of Experience,* he writes about stories: "Stories are
necessary to weave a web of meaning within which we can live. We all live
in story worlds. They create for us the atmosphere of understandability that
seems necessary for ordinary survival" (Mair, 1989a, p. 277). He goes in
depth to explore what stories are about, what they are useful for, their place
in our living and more. Stories appear to be a sort of *Leitmotiv,* as we say, a
leading motif which is indicative of one's inner urges as well of ones outer
appearance, one's place in this world. It might be considered as an all-
comprising construct with a wide range of convenience which, however,
regrettably sometimes has already assumed the quality of a worn-out metaphor.

Now, I should like to take that construct to use it in a more concretistic way. I
have noticed that many people have crystallised their experiences by way of
constructing stories: stories about events, adventures, people they knew,
minor or major incidents, and accidents. I think this kind of story is a means
of organising anticipations. I suppose that by this type of construing, commonality and sociality are more easily achieved than by a discourse on a
more abstract level: "This happened once, so it can and will happen again."

*I remember a western movie where the hero, I think it was James Stewart,
accompanied every second incident or interaction with a story of the type: 'I
knew a guy in Wichita, Kansas, who used to sleep with his gun under his*

pillow, too...' thus making predictions about what would happen to his partner.

I have noticed that I tend to use this tool myself frequently in everyday life, and of course I use it today. I believe that when using a foreign language, telling stories is less liable to misunderstanding because it is easier to catch the spirit of a story than to follow a more abstract, however elaborate, discourse.

The kind of storytelling I have in mind is not about 'stories of a lifetime', like Audrey Hepburn's in *A Nun's Story* or Elsa Morante's great novel *La Storia*. What I mean are small-scale stories, and I should like to call this kind of Everyman's psychology 'psychology as *short-story* telling'.

Conversational psychology

Let us look back now to the section on sociolinguistic aspects of communication. When I am engaged in a discussion with several English-speaking people, I am painfully aware of my limitations in vocabulary, my inability to follow the curves and ups and downs and to's and fro's of the path of discourse. And when I am trying to engage in the talking, I realise that there is an astounding similarity in my speaking to what Bernstein (1990) termed the *restricted code:* I use short, often incomplete sentences, prefer nouns, ignore grammatical rules, apply stereotyped formulas like 'you know', try to use gestures and pantomime to communicate, and so on.

I remember travelling in Greece once, and somewhere in the centre of the Peloponnes peninsula we met an old shepherd who had a not very large flock of sheep in the valley next to the place where we were camping We could say no more than 'Kalimeran' but he spoke fluent Greek and apparently tried to convey something to us. He made a gesture in the direction of his sheep and repeated what we couldn't grasp. All of a sudden he changed his tactics: he spoke without any tone, but still spoke, with exaggerated grimaces. Still without success. We later came to the conclusion that he must have construed us as deaf and resorted to the proper way of communication to the deaf.

A similar event was reported by a German writer, Erhart Kästner, who during the war served in the occupation forces in Greece, but whenever possible left his unit to explore the classic landscape. He once met a Greek shepherd who couldn't make himself understood, exactly like ours 30 years later. But this one resorted to talking overly loud - he took the stranger not for deaf but only for hard of hearing.

Now let me quote Miller Mair again:

   If am not understood (e.g. when in a foreign country most of us are

foreigners to most others!) I will be lonely isolated, an outsider; a
spectator; and not a participant I am liable to begin to lose a sense of
reality feel frightened, become hungry for contact To find someone
who speaks your language con be an immense relief even though in
normal circumstances you have little in common.

If no one understands your language (what you mean, what your
meaning is or might be) then you are likely to have to shrink You may
6nly stumble a few incoherent words. Any competence you might have
had vanishes. You are reduced to a state of foolishness, childishness,
idiocy (Mair 1989a, p. 216*)*

Precisely that happened to us and to the German writer in Greece, and it is not far from what many people may experience at an international conference.

Miller Mair in his book advocates what he terms a *conversational psychology*. The outlines seem still not very precise, but I understand that it is to be a psychology concerned with the people involved. Miller says: "It will be a psychology of understanding rather than a psychology of information about (understanding and the struggle for different understandings is likely to be central to any notion of conversation)" (Mair, 1989a, p. 216). It is about listening, thinking aloud, talking, asking, telling. It sounds almost Socratian.

Why I quote these ideas in the given context is because I think that the idiocy and the isolation the noncommunicating foreigner is likely to experience can only be broken up by a conversational approach. Please have in mind that those of you who have English as a native tongue will experience this much less than we others because of the aforementioned role of the English language in the modern world. For because of this most people will try to make themselves understood by using English, however deficient the attempts may be - like I do in this address.

What that means for the present occasion, the International Congress on Personal Construct Psychology I shall try to explicate in the next section.

Constructive internationalism

Why do we attend congresses? The decision matrix to do so has to be made several times a year and is undoubtedly grounded in a number of probably hierarchically organised constructs. In Table 2 is a list of some of my constructs about why to go to a conference.

How about going to a PCP conference, especially an international one?

My constructs about PCP people can best be put in the form of a little story:

When attending my first international congress, I had an experience which puzzled me quite a bit. It was during one of the plenary lectures which were probably intended to give sort of a solid round to build theorising on. But it turned out to be basic statements by Kelly projected on overhead transparencies, with questions following of the kind: what did Kelly mean by this or what does this give us today? It reminded me of the exegesis procedures of catechism lectures (which I fortunately was not forced to attend as a child). And it was not the iron corollaries that were analysed that way. After that, I thought (and said to people I already knew better at that time): Am I about to join the wrong sect?

However, my friends told me: "Wait till the workshops start, and you will feel better in the small group atmosphere prevailing there." And that was true.

Tab. 2: *My constructs about congresses (Decision Matrix)*

dull	-	interesting
large	-	small
anonymous	-	intimate
arrogant people	-	empathetic people
ego presentation	-	interested in others
interpersonal discourse	-	marketplace for gossip
personal interests in participants	-	marketing for jobs
rivalry	-	cooperation and exchange
people want to be seen	-	people want to meet each other
open discussion about the future paths of the art	-	defending the Holy Grail
looking for common interests	-	intrigues to carry through own interests/advantages
get conference grants	-	got to pay myself
meet old friends	-	don't know anybody
spare time for leisure activities	-	full-packed schedule
insiders only	-	everybody is welcome
'congressual' language prevailing	-	multilingual communication facilitated
ample space for discussion	-	mainly listening
loose time schedule	-	tightly knit program schedule
got to travel very far	-	travel around the corner

My impressions or constructs have been validated since many times. I have attended quite a number of national and international conferences, congresses, and formal and informal meetings in the realms of psychology and medicine, and most of them are dominated by the happy few who are in possession of the resources of any kind, not the least the power to speak whenever they want to speak and to say whatever they want to say. In PCP conferences, I noticed that not only the founding fathers (who are apparently sons - and daughters - themselves) and their immediate offsprings seize the word, but that, compared to other disciplines, relatively many people engage unaffectedly in the discussions. I guess that may partly be due to the fact that academic honours are rarely won by practising PCP or publishing in this field, and consequently the people who attend the conferences are really interested in the matter and in other people and what they have to say. So, the fundamental requirements for a conversational psychology seem to be given.

That's how the notion of *constructive internationalism* came to my mind. You will have noticed the allusion to constructive alternativism. Another association may be something like *proletarian internationalism.* And finally, one might think of the submerged pole of *nonconstructive* or *destructive internationalism* which some people see in what certain spiritual and worldly forces have been practising over the centuries and still do. And finally, *constructive imperialism* could be understood as a policy of - in many instances unintentionally - supplying constructs to the rest of the world.

What would be the conclusions? Equal right for the German language, or for Italian, German, and Spanish? Simultaneous translations from and into German, French, Spanish, Dutch, Italian, Norwegian, Zimbabwean - or how many languages are represented at a given PCP congress? Stencilled handouts with lengthy summaries in 15 languages (or eventually 115?). Installing Esperanto as *the* congress idiom?

I am not pleading for equal right for the German language, or for Italian, German, and Spanish, as mother tongues of an - at present time - substantial number of personal constructivists. This very fundamentalist idea of course would not be practicable. And it would transfer the problem to about 500 other languages that would be excluded.

Let me make it personal again. With my restricted competence in English, I am generally able to follow a lecture, to discuss some not-too-complicated issues, in English. Provided the psychomotor speed of lips and larynx of the speakers is not too high, there is sufficient time to adapt to the personal meanings, dialects, idiosyncratic verbal behaviours, and so on.

However, in a discussion of, say, more than five people, I have noticed that English speakers from different origins, take Boston, Oklahoma, Scotland, London, or New South Wales for example, tend to speak like they were at home at their native camp-fire, irrespective of who else is present.

Now, when I first communicated some of my ideas to other people, in this case British, they complained that they did not understand some of the Australians, many of the Americans, and so on. And I was told that British authors who had submitted manuscripts to American journals experienced what they felt to be censorship concerning some grammatical or linguistic details that were considered un-English (to avoid the term un-American). This gave me the idea that my problem was not only a personal one, but one that pertained to some other non-English (or as it seems, even native English) speakers, too.

Constructivists generally stress the importance of seeing the other (the client, the patient, the pupil, the manager to be counselled) as being a human being, with his/her own construct system, which has to be accepted and respected and even honoured (if not welcomed), and I have already heard that several times during this conference. How about fellow constructivists? I do not advocate abandoning the prevailing practice, but to be aware of the other people - if you care for what we have to say.

The concluding story

Let me close with a historical fantasy.

I was told that there is a legend (or maybe it is a fact) that at one time in the history of the United States of America a decision had to be made about whether English or German was to be the language of the Union. The assembly voted with a majority of one, which ironically was a German-speaking American. The results are known. However, had the decision been different, then the mainlands of PCP would be the following (see Figure 2):

- *die Vereinigten Staaten von Nordamerika (the US),*

- *Deutschland (also known as Germany),*

- *Österreich (you may prefer Felix Austria,), und*

- *die Schweiz (Switzerland).*

And the godfather of the movement would be one

GEORG KELLER.

Fig. 2. *The alternative map of Personal Construct Psychology (PCP).*

References

Balint, E., & Norell, J.S. (Eds.). (1973). *Six minutes for the patient: Interactions in general practice consultation.* London: Tavitrock.

Balint, E., & Norell, J.S. (Ms.) (1975). *Fünf Minuten pro Patient: Eine Studie über die Interaktionen in der ärztlichen Allgemeinpraxis.* Frankfurt: Suhrkamp.

Bannister, D., & Fransella, F. (1981). *Der Mensch als Forscher* [Inquiring Man). Münster: Aschendorff.

Bernstein, B. (1990). *Class code and control: Vol. 4. The structuring of pedagogic discourse.* London: Routledge.

Fisher, D. (1989, August). *Language use: A constructivist view of politics and morality.* Paper presented at the 8th International Congress on Personal Construct Psychology. Assisi, Italy.

Kelly, G.A. (1962). Europe's matrix of decision. *Nebraska Symposium on Motivation, 10,* 83-123. *(reprinted in this volume)*

Mair, M. (1 989a). *Between psychology and psychotherapy: A poetics of experience.* London: Routledge.

Mair, M. (1989b). Kelly, Bannister, and a story-telling psychology. *Intrernational Journal of Personal Construct Psychology 2;* 1—14.

Mair, M. (1990). Telling psychological tales. *International Journal of Personal Construct Psychology 3;* 121—135.

Webster's New School of Office Dictionary (1960). Greenwich, CT: Fawcett.

How are meanings negotiated? Commonality, sociality, and the travel of ideas

Devi Jankowicz, Dorota Dobosz-Bourne

Devi: *I first realised the personal relevance of an interest in cross-cultural communication when I attended a paper Jörn gave at the 10th International Congress on Personal Construct Psychology held in Townsville in Australia[25]. This dear,* infuriating *man made his point about the primacy of language dramatically clear by delivering the first 5 minutes of his paper in German, leaving myself and the other Anglos in the audience nodding sagely while reflecting, in some desperation, on the obvious disadvantage of being native speakers of the world's most popular tongue...*

Dorota: *The personal relevance of my own interest started when as a sixteen year old, I was sent to an Austrian school with a basic command of the German language. Contrary to my expectations, a command of the German language was not enough to enable one to communicate smoothly in the dialect spoken in Salzburg. Ten years later I arrived in the UK to begin my doctoral studies and re-discovered a need for rapid language acquisition if the results of my research were to be comprehensible to my examiners...*

Devi and Dorota: *...but both of us have this valuable thing, current fluency in a second language. While we were raised in two different cultures, we have spoken Polish from birth, and here we are writing in English as we work in that language. Our personal histories inform our research interests, which overlap with Jörn's and which concern the ways in which ideas travel across cultural boundaries. We specialise in the relationship between the west and Central/Eastern Europe (C/EE), in the transfer of ideas about the market economy into the various post-command economies of that region, Poland in particular.*

Much has changed since the early 1990s, when that conference took place. Perhaps the biggest difference lies in way in which we construe our own involvement, as scholars in a community which operates across cultural boundaries, in the study of the process by which ideas cross cultural boundaries. And we have become rather more reflective about the whole business.

---

[25] Reprinted in this volume (p. 104-121*) (Ed.)*

We regard knowledge transfer as something in which mutual sense and meaning have to be carefully *negotiated* because sense and meaning are not global or absolute. This issue arises after the vocabulary has been translated; *after* we have, supposedly, understood the other person's basic utterances. To the extent that people in different cultures understand the world differently, they must expend deliberate effort in trying to come to terms with each other's meanings, over and above their translated vocabularies, if they are to collaborate successfully. So the study of knowledge transfer becomes, in part, the study of the ways in which the processes of *sociality* supplement *commonality*, but on the scale of a whole society rather than on the individual level which Kelly originally had in mind, when he published *The Psychology of Personal Constructs* in 1955.

This process is bi-directional, each party operating within its own context of interested stakeholders (people, organisations and institutions) which support, but also constrain, each negotiating position. The participants mutually reflect on this process, and are increasingly aware that the meanings they create can only be understood through the network of ontological and epistemological presuppositions called culture. And cultures vary, so that meanings which are possible in one culture may be dissimilar, or indeed impossible, in another culture.

So how *is* it possible to make progress across different cultures? What do we need to know about how mutually sensible and useful meanings reflexively emerge? Let's examine a model by which the travel of ideas can be described, and use it to interpret some empirical data. The argument is illustrated with examples drawn from a series of ethnographic interviews reported in Dobosz and Jankowicz (2002). This dealt with a particular case: the ways in which the concept of 'Quality' is construed in two cultures, and how the idea of 'Quality' in car manufacturing travelled cross-culturally, from the USA, to Japan, to Germany and the UK, and, finally, to Poland.

The Czarniawska - Joerges Model

A brief outline of the basic assertions of the model (Czarniawska & Joerges, 1996) as follows

An *idea* exists within a *cultural field* in which it is embedded; it takes its meaning from associations available in that particular culture. The idea is expressed through corresponding *objects*. These objects are utilised in particular *actions* in a societal milieu, and the more important behaviour becomes standardised and regulated through the process of *institutionalisation*. In order for an idea to travel by one objectified means or other (a radio broadcast, an utterance, a book, a training manual, an artefact such as a piece of artwork or equipment) it has to be *dis-embedded* from the various cultural assumptions which those processes have brought about. It then becomes understood and utilised within a new culture only to the extent that it can be *re-embedded* into the ongoing processes which apply to objects, actions, and institutions of its kind *in the new culture*. Each arrow in the figure stands for an act of translation– linguistic, behavioural, social and institutional.

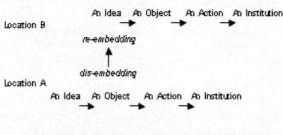

Each arrow stands for a process of translation. The Object is dis-embedded from one cultural matrix and has to be re-embedded into the pre-existing matrix of its new location.

Fig. 1: *The 'Travels of Ideas' model, Czarniawska & Joerges (1996)*

This model offers a convenient analytic framework for any knowledge transfer activity, suggesting a number of questions which need addressing if the transfer is to be successful.

- Firstly, *the nature of the two cultural fields themselves.* Czarniawska's model suggests a focus for our attention on the similarities or dissimilarities that exist in the *beliefs* which govern comparable action, and in the *values* which drive corresponding institutions. To the extent that different pressures, stemming from these differences in construing in the two cultures, constrain action, we observe a lessened commonality of action. In short, what does each culture find easy to do, what is difficult or impossible, and what can be emulated because the pattern of constraints in one's own culture is similar. What can be done in one's own culture that can't in the other, because one's own culture does not contain such constraints?

- Articulation of a relationship between two cultures also depends on *the pre-existing relationship between those two cultures*. What compatibilities and incompatibilities arise from the history between the two countries? How have ideas translated in the past: through diffusion, imitation, explicit proselytisation, or through domination? The fate of an idea travelling between England and Ireland, Denmark and Sweden, Russia and Afghanistan, Turkey and Greece is likely to be different in each case, in more or less subtle ways. The constraints which operate may be the outcome of centuries of sociality– the results of the ways in which each of the two cultures regards itself after deliberate comparison of itself, to itself-as-seen-through-the-other's eyes. A particular historical relationship between two cultures can constrain the relationships each maintains with other cultures. Stroinska (2001: 13-14), for example, reports that until the end of Soviet economic dominance in Poland, it was impossible to translate Klemperer's book on the language of the Third Reich into Polish because of the similarity of many of the metaphors and figures used in Nazi rhetoric to the metaphors being currently used in communist literary style.

- *The complexity of the translation process* needs to be taken into account. How many cultural boundaries are involved, and what is the 'cultural distance' which ideas need to travel? As Barkema et al. (1996) have pointed out, a joint venture between two companies within one nation state already involves the crossing of a cultural boundary– that which exists between two organisational cultures. A joint venture involving companies in two different countries collaborating in one of those two countries involves two units of distance, one being the organisational difference and the second being the difference in national cultures. The same joint venture for manufacture and sales in a third country offers a third unit of distance, and so on. Czarniawska's model is not limited to a pair of cultures, but provides for onwards travel from location to location.

- Finally, and most importantly, *the act of translation itself*, which forms the focus of this paper and from which everything else follows. Some ideas are easily translated, and some translate with difficulty; low commonality results in greater difficulties for the attempt at sociality.

No two cultures are identical, but no two cultures are completely different. A consideration of the nature of the cultural field, the pre-existing relationships, the cultural distance, and the acts of translation as they pertain to the particular ideas being transferred in a given, planned collaboration would suggest what scope for successful transfer exists at a given time for the idea in its original form; and what changes in presentation of the idea might be feasible as the negotiation over meaning takes place.

The translation process: language as an encoding system

Clearly, for this negotiation to take place the two parties need to understand each other and, if they do not share a common language, translation of the language in which the idea is expressed is a central part of the travel of that idea. That was the first conundrum Jörn created for the Anglos in Townsville. But, really, that was the easy bit, for, as well as being a medium of *communication*, language is, much more importantly, a medium of *representation*. It is a system of tokens and rules for encoding (representing, recording, reporting) experience in a particular culture. If the nature and range of experiences in that culture differ from another, (and in the case of the west *vis-à-vis* the C/EE countries, we are talking about 500 years of history rather than a mere 50 years of Marxism), so will the language. The vocabulary will be different, and so some words will be missing, and won't translate (Jankowicz, 2002; Holden & Cooper, 1994). This is the relatively minor problem, for it is always possible to substitute some sort of alternative, or a more extended locution, or a carefully defined neologism. However, the structure of the language, the rules by which phenomena are noticed and placed in relationship to each other (in other words, construed!), will also differ, and this is rather more serious. Different cultures notice different things standing out as meaningful figures against the background of the phenomenal flow. Since meaning is a matter of associations and relationships between ideas, different cultures may differ over what constitutes 'an event'; where they agree in its identification, they may nevertheless give different meanings to the 'same event', and over time, evolve rules of grammar, orthography, figure, metaphor and idiom by which to do so (Guthrie, 1991; Jankowicz, 1999).

Another way of saying this is that experience in one culture does not match experience in another. What are recognised as distinct, nameable events in one culture may be regarded differently, or even be unnoticed, (I would not go so far as Whorf and claim them to be *unnoticeable*: Whorf & Carroll, 1974), in another. As an adaptive system which grows, develops, and flexes over time in the light of events, in order to encode those events, the language of each of the two cultures will, however, slice up the phenomenal flow differently. If at any one moment an utterance in one language is translated into another, there may be nothing that can be transferred, and meaning evaporates in translation.

Of course, such differences are rarely total, always a matter of degree, and the extent of this overlap can be readily described. Similarity of meaning is a function of two language properties:

-   the web of associations that each culture recognises in the terms being translated

-   *and* the extent to which similar constructs exist in the two languages.

To illustrate, using English-Polish translation as the example. When we say that something is 'Good', for example, we only know what's meant if we know the full construct being referred to: if we're talking about 'Good versus Evil', or 'Good versus Poor' (as in the case of a student essay we're grading), in which the word 'Good' denotes something entirely different. When we translate each of these two constructs into Polish, we can observe the similarity of meanings in both languages by looking for similar associations and, as Figure 2 shows, the translation of 'Good versus Evil' is unproblematic; there are plenty of similar associations, *and* the construct exists in both languages.

Fig. 2: *'Good and Evil' is not a problem!*

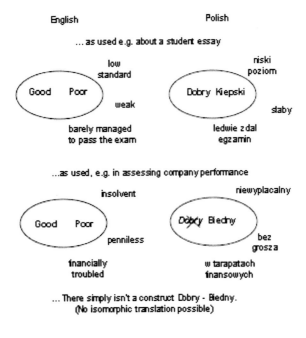

Fig. 3: *But 'Good and Poor' certainly is!*

Figure 3 indicates that there is a problem with 'Good versus Poor', however, because there are two senses in which one can use 'Good versus Poor' in English but only one in Polish. You can describe a student essay and company performance in terms of this construct in English, but when you speak of company performance in Polish, there is no such thing as 'Good versus Poor', with the same associations as in English! (In fact, in Polish, you'd use the construct which applies to student essays when describing company performance.)

Translation of the idea of quality in car assembly

An illustration of Czarniawska's model in use is provided by focusing on the idea of 'Quality' as applied in manufacturing, specifically, how the idea of 'Quality' travelled in its final stage between two General Motors assembly plants: Vauxhall Motors (UK), and the Opel Works in Gliwice, Poland. The examples draw on the fuller account given in Dobosz & Jankowicz (2002) which outlines the results of Dorota's ethnographic interviews with Polish and English managers responsible for introducing, negotiating and managing western ideas of 'Quality' into the Polish car manufacturing industry.

Nature of the field itself: beliefs governing action

Firstly, it is clear that 'Quality' is not something which was absent in Polish industry and only 'arrived' when western manufacturing and assembly techniques (themselves strongly shaped by Japanese methods) were imported into Poland during the 1990s. However, the existing idea was mainly confined to engineering specifications, and to the basic standards and regulations governing food processing. The various additional notions of overall finish, presentation and packaging, reliability, after-sales, or quality of service were absent. 'Pre-War craftsmanship', and the idea of Stakhanovite personal energy in productivity imported from Russia after the war, had iconic status, each grounded in a different cultural era but both expressing the belief that 'Quality' was a matter of individual talent, skill, and motivation. *"If you care, if you draw on your talents and skills and show flair, you will produce quality products and services"*.

This belief is grounded in Polish culture, as the language indicates. Figure 4 draws on a dictionary technique first outlined in Jankowicz (1994) to demonstrate that the Polish terms expressive of 'Quality' focus on the nature of the object which is produced, as a result of talent and motivated effort– much as in English usage. What Polish culture lacked, until it was imported, was the notion that anyone, not especially motivated, without any particular flair or creativity beyond the ability to follow instructions in a trained manner, was capable of producing 'Quality' – because when the manufacturing process is appropriately arranged, 'Quality' becomes an inherent property of a set of assembly, testing, and operations management *procedures*, rather than being a property of an article manufactured in a skilled and motivated way. "Quality isn't a matter of whim, effort, or flair. If you follow these particular procedures *you cannot help but* produce the quality products or services which are our normal standard".

	Three meanings of the English word		
A. English original	Quality	Quality	Quality
B. Polish trans.* of A (The Pole is informed that these are the meaning inherent in the English)	Jakosc	Zaleta, lub Cecha	Ranga
C. English back-trans.* of B (I am informing you what these terms denote to the Pole)	Quality, kind, nature	Virtue, quality, merit, advantage, or Hallmark, attribute, character	Social rank

- The emphasis in the Polish is on inherent characteristics
- The usage as a collective term for people of a higher social ranking, is absent in Polish

* All translations using Bulas (1967)

Fig. 4: *The Polish equivalent of 'Quality'*

How did the new belief take root? It seems that the time was ripe to redefine beliefs about 'Quality' in terms other than motivational. The prior belief was that there were no employee incentives worth bothering about –

Czy sie stoi czy sie lezy, dwa tysiace sie nalezy

(You're owed the same wages whether you remain upright or whether you sleep on the job)

was a popular shopfloor saying during the era of the command economy when all wages were centrally determined regardless of local performance– and so long as it was culturally construed as motivational in nature, 'Quality' was pointless because of the absence of incentive.

The suggestion that 'Quality' resides in procedures made it possible to engage in 'Quality' in a different and meaningful way, independently of the issue of incentives. And of course the employees were open to new procedures since they were taken on in a green-field situation in which the entire

129

production process, even for those who came from pre-existing Polish car assembly operations, was in itself being redefined.

Nature of the field itself: values driving the institutionalisation process

Introducing these procedures required a redefinition of the role of manager, from someone who directs and controls, to someone who leads, facilitates and coaches. This, Dorota discovered in her UK interviews at Vauxhall, had occurred in the 1980s, the macho style common to the UK motor industry of the time being gradually tempered with the more participative style that the new working procedures require (Wickens, 1987). The Polish equivalents of 'management' (see Figure 5) have always been culturally regarded as directive and authoritative (Maczynski, 1994; Rakowska, 1995; Kruzela et al., 1996) regardless of which industry is involved and, under the command economy, there was a strong tendency towards a uniformity of organisational culture (Czarniawska, 1986), which suggests that the directive style of management was universal. It is arguable that the notion of a management style– that the way one manages is open to variation – arrived only with the new practices introduced by the western companies as they arrived in Poland.

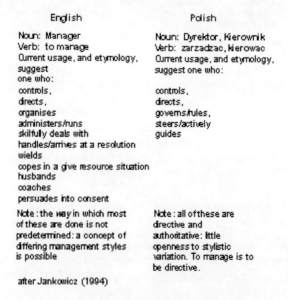

English	Polish
Noun: Manager Verb: to manage Current usage, and etymology, suggest one who:	Noun: Dyrektor, Kierownik Verb: zarzadzac, kierowac Current usage, and etymology, suggest one who:
controls, directs, organises administers/runs skilfuly deals with handles/arrives at a resolution wields copes in a give resource situation husbands coaches persuades into consent	controls, directs, governs/rules, steers/actively guides
Note : the way in which most of these are done is not predetermined: a concept of differing management styles is possible	Note : all of these are directive and authoritative: little openness to stylistic variation. To manage is to be directive.

after Jankowicz (1994)

Fig. 5: *Polish and English meanings for 'Management'*

The concept of management style carries a variety of value assumptions. At a crude level, a naive Organisation Development perspective exalts participative styles and devalues directive styles, while at a rather more sophisticated level, all styles are acceptable and it is the flexibility with which style can be adjusted contingent on resources, situation and employee needs which is positively valued (e.g. Fiedler, 1967; House & Mitchell, 1974). And so, it is now possible for management at Opel Polska to say "do it our way or else" as before, but also to say "we will help you, and coach you, to do it this way" and, moreover "as you become familiar with these ways, we will encourage you to provide your own ideas about how it might be improved: you tell us, since your experience at the sharp end is more valuable than ours".

In the meanwhile, and during the training period, the English word 'manager' was adopted (as it has been across a wide range of industries in Poland) as a neologism, spelt according to Polish orthographic convention as '*menedzer*' in order to carry the additional meanings, absent in the equivalent Polish terms, required for those situations in which alternatives to a directive style were required.

Pre-existing relationship between the two cultures

It seems that the new working practices are particularly effective at Opel Polska. During the last year, the plant achieved the highest level of quality of all the European General Motors plants. And it is clear that the way the products are being made, and involvement in their manufacture, carries deep cultural significance. Historically, Poland has always attempted to counterbalance its location between more powerful neighbours by looking to the west (France, UK, America, Canada) for cultural support, reference and legitimation.

It is apparent from Dorota's interviews that possession of a Polish Opel, or involvement in its manufacture, carries powerful symbolic meaning. It represents a renewal of pre-existing links with the west which had been sundered during the period of the command economy. A vehicle built according to the highest global standards associated with western capitalism, using assembly and testing procedures which represent the cutting edge at a global level, is construed by both employees and customers as the final stage of the construction of a post-command economy, en route to Polish participation in the global economy. It is contrasted with the gimcrack vehicle assembled using slipshod working practices during the period of stagnation of the command economy years, and with the palpably inadequate way in which cars were sold, maintained and serviced during that time, when the purchaser waiting for decades before a car became available for purchase, spare parts were nonexistent, and an extensive network of small-scale, privately-owned, and expensive repair and panel-beating shops was the only alternative to a state sector in which prices were cheap but service delays inordinate. Thus the arrival of the idea of 'Quality' from the West, as represented by the Opel

Polska plant, comes to stand for national change and rebirth, entirely in tune with the pre-existing aspirations of national identity.

One of Dorota's English managers, working in the Polish plant, expressed this very well:

> *I think... It's difficult for me to say this because I'm not Polish you know. You'd have to talk to some local Polish people but I think, most Polish people in Opel Polska wanted us to be successful because they want Poland to be successful. And Opel Polska represents the new Poland. It's what Poland is and wants to be in the future rather than, you know, where it was before when the post-command economic reforms happened. So a lot of people identify what's happening nationally in the country with companies like Opel Polska.*

The complexity of the translation process

The idea of 'Quality' in car assembly is widely travelled. The new production methods came from Japan (some of them via Korea) before they impinged on assembly practices in the UK and Germany; and that while properly regarded as 'the Japanese style of manufacturing', they stem from the original period of American support for Japanese reconstruction in the immediate post-War period (Deming, 1989). In Barkema's terms, many cultural boundaries have been crossed: at least 5 national boundaries, and several boundaries of organisational culture, as different manufacturers developed their own variants of the Japanese procedures, passing on information about each others' ways whenever managers changed jobs between companies within the industry.

The idea (itself a large compilation of detailed practices) followed a complex route in its travels. A series of mappings between object and idea took place, a series of complex disembeddings and re-embeddings, the rate of change in different countries being governed by the extent to which local translation of objects into actions, and institutionalisation of those actions, progresssed.

The act of translation itself

At each stage, the local disembedding and re-embedding needs to be examined in detail. We can illustrate the process by looking at the way in which meanings were constructed through language, drawing on some examples from Dorota's empirical work. The objects which, literally, travelled from site to site were of three kinds:

- written manuals describing procedures, technical specifications, training requirements and the like,

- specialised measuring equipment used in assembly and testing,

- staff charged with a special mission to foster and disseminate the new procedures, and localised discoveries of good practice that could be transferred onwards.

The *disembedding* process involved the provision of statements of objectives, purpose and values present in the originating location which it was necessary to adopt if action using the object itself were to be effective; *embedding* was intended to occur largely through the training of newly-hired employees. One of the most important factors in the embedding process was the opportunity created by a very low selection ratio (2,500 jobs available for over 40,000 applicants) to choose employees whose age, job history, and personal attitudes suggested an openness to the new ideas. It is certainly true that the economic situation (and more particularly, high unemployment), is a harsh but significant factor which contributes to the advent and travel of new ideas. Those who are open to new meanings are chosen, and those who are not remain unemployed.

Re-embedding was also accomplished by a deliberate use of language to compel attention to the novelty, difference, and importance of some of the actions required by the new quality procedures. As with the Polonisation of the foreign term 'menedzer' so that all of the meaning, necessary to the importation of a flexible management style, could be captured, so with other neologisms such as *Kaizen, Andon*, and *Gemba.*.

There were no pre-existing Polish terms that carried the precise procedural implications of these Japanese terms, which symbolise the meanings of 'continuous improvement', 'calling attention to defects', and 'turning principles into experience' respectively. The activities and values underlying the terms were carefully defined, but they were presented to employees in their Japanese form, less as a convenient shorthand for actions through which 'Quality' is defined, but more as a way of compelling attention to the nature of 'Quality'. As a UK manager who had taken part in that training commented:

> *We don't use Polish words in a lot of occasions. In the same way in the UK they don't.* Kaizen *is* Kaizen. Andon *is* Andon. *That works, in my opinion, really well because it's a new concept for most of the people, so why pretend it is something that is already in Poland?* Andon *is* Andon. *And we tell people honestly in the presentation "This word has no meaning in English. It means 'alarm' in Japanese". So, automatically you have this image – this is a new technique.*

Re-embedding was also achieved by making use of financial incentive schemes to reward employees who proposed effective ways to Kaizen their work: 'seizing the opportunity' to assist the travel of an idea in this case implies that a formal reward scheme is set up and that funds are set aside for this purpose. Notice what is being incentivised: not generic 'energy' associated with quality as motivation, but specific attention devoted to activities directed at problem-solving which increases 'Quality'.

Such actions have been strongly institutionalised, by developing 'Kaizen stations' along the assembly line, to which employees with a record of successful Kaizen can be transferred permanently, their role being to develop and trial new instrumentation or variations in procedure designed to maintain the rate of improvement.

An example of an attempt at re-embedding which clashed with the pre-existing cultural field is provided by the introduction of uniforms for all staff managerial and shop-floor, an attempted institutionalisation of the quality-related idea of 'single status for all employees'. The female employees took particularly strong exception to being unable to wear their own clothes at work, and production came to a halt until the uniforms were re-presented by management as having important symbolic value, as well as the more utilitarian function of preserving the employees' own clothes.

The nature of the symbol is interesting, though. Personal work-clothing and accessories (e.g. shirts, protective gloves, soap, towels) had been issued to employees in the days of the command economy. The objects in question had exchange value, and were seen as one of the small perks of certain occupations, which could be sold on to friends outside of the place of employment. And so, when uniforms which had to be worn at all times were issued at Opel Polska, far from symbolising the single status associated with a quality-driven organisation, the issue of uniforms was, at first, interpreted as a reduction in employee benefits.

Finally, the translation of 'Quality' has been institutionalised in the form of key job roles. Some employees are designated as International Service Persons, who are thoroughly trained in General Motors quality procedures and are loaned from their parent company to fill critical skills gaps and, in doing so, bring new quality ideas and actions from other GM locations where those procedures have already been thoroughly institutionalised.

Conclusion

Some time ago, Bourdieu warned us of

> *misunderstandings, borrowings removed from their context and reinterpreted, admiring initiation and disdainful aloofness – these are all signs familiar to specialists on the situations that arise when cultures meet... any action for the handing on of a culture necessarily implies an affirmation of the value of the culture imparted (and, correlatively,*

an implicit or explicit depreciation of other possible cultures) (Bourdieu, 1971: 198).

It would appear that a culture can be handed on in a way which is not denigratory, and does not require an intrusive and usually only partly successful internalisation of foreign values, provided the ideas in question can be presented in a way that maximises the compatibilities of meaning between the two cultures.

In summary, what strategies are available for increasing success in the transfer of ideas? What might one do to facilitate sociality activities as meanings are mutually negotiated?

- Couch the idea in language which as far as possible maps onto pre-existing meanings in both cultures, as an aid to the negotiation of a mutually comprehensible meaning. *You can't put yourself into the other's shoes if the shoes don't fit.*

- Particularly, avoid constructs in one culture which have no easy correspondence in the other; this implies mutual exploration of the meanings that *are* available. *Gradually, start making new designs for shoes, together.*

- Clarify the meaning of action in each culture: what assumptions exist in both cultures which influence the ways in which objects are used in action, and the ways in which actions might feasibly be institutionalised (e.g. is 'Quality' a motivational or a procedural entity?) *Agree on how the shoes might be made.*

- In both cultures, identify the values addressed by the actions and institutions being proposed; if there is a mismatch, what alternative values can be appealed to? *What sort of shoes ought to be made?*

- Pre-existing cultural preferences and styles may pose a problem in joint ventures between existing organisations with intact and incompatible organisational cultures; in the case of green-field operations, build appropriate cultures by selecting employees open to such influence. *Take advantage of new shoe-making materials, locally available.*

- Recognise the compatibilities which exist in the previous relationship between the two cultures; what local aspirations can be addressed by entraining the objectives of the venture onto those local values? *If we don't like trainers and you don't like sandals, can we agree on the good old-fashioned leather shoe that Mum wanted us to wear?*

- Identify the symbolic value of the objects and actions through which the idea is expressed in each culture, and in order to achieve a successful institutionalisation, choose those objects and actions which share similar meanings; if these are dissimilar, are they at least compatible? *Is* ein Pantoffel *a* gemütlich *sort of object in German? It's certainly very* comfy *in English. Very well then, let us collaborate in the manufacture of slippers.*

Car assembly or shoe manufacture? It may be that the same rules of cross-cultural sociality apply.

References

Barkema, H. G., J. H. J. Bell, Pennings, J.M. (1996). Foreign entry, cultural barriers, and learning. *Strategic Management Journal* 17, 151-166.

Bourdieu, P. (1971). Systems of education and systems of thought. *Knowledge and control: new directions for the sociology of education*. M. F. D. Young. London, Collier Macmillan.

Bulas, K., Thomas L.L., Whitfield F.J. (1967) *The Koscuszko Foundation Dictionary, English-Polish (vol. 1) and Polish-English (vol. 2)*. New York: Kosciuszko Foundation.

Czarniawska, B. (1986). The management of meaning in the Polish crisis. *Journal of Management Studies* 23(3): 313-331.

Czarniawska, B.,, Joerges, B. (1999) Travels of ideas. in Czarniawska, B. & G. Sevon, (eds.) *Translating organizational change*. Berlin: De Gruyter.

Deming, W. E. (1989). *Foundation for the management of quality in the western world*, Perigee Books.

Dobosz D., Jankowicz A.D. (2000) Knowledge transfer of the western concept of quality. *Human Resource Development International* 5, 3, 353-367.

Fiedler, F. E. (1967). *A contingency theory of leadership effectiveness*. New York, McGraw-Hill.

Guthrie, A. F. (1991). Intuiting the process of another: symbolic, rational transformations of experience. *International Journal of Personal Construct Psychology* 4(3): 273-279.

Holden, N., Cooper, C. (1994). Russian managers as learners and receivers of western know-how. *Management Learning* 25(4): 503-522.

House, R. J., Mitchell, T. R. (1974). Path-goal theory of leadership. *Journal of Contemporary Business* 3: 81-97.

Jankowicz, A. D. (1994). The new journey to Jerusalem: mission and meaning in the managerial crusade to eastern Europe. *Organization Studies* 15(4): 479-507.

Jankowicz, A. D. (1999). Planting a paradigm in Central Europe: do we graft, or must we breed the rootstock anew? *Management Learning* 30(3): 281-299.

Jankowicz, A. D. (2002) Cross-cultural knowledge transfer: translation as a mutual negotiation of disparate meanings in Chiari, G., Nuzzo, M. L. (eds.) *Proceedings of the 6th Conference of the European Personal Construct Association*, Florence, March.

Kelly, G.A. (1955). *The Psychology of Personal Constructs* New York: Norton.

Kruzela, P., Smith, P.B., Grobleska, B., Halasova, D. (1996). Event management in transformational context: management styles in the Czech, Slovak and Polish Republics. *3rd Annual Workshop on Cross-Cultural Management*, Henley on Thames, European Institute for Advanced Studies in Management, Henley Management College UK.

Maczynski, J. (1994). Culture and leadership styles: a comparison of Polish, Austrian and U.S. managers. *Polish Psychological Bulletin* 25(4): 303-315.

Rakowska, A. (1995). Managerial styles and gender differences in Poland. *Labour Process Conference*, University of Central Lancashire, April.

Stroinska, M. (2001). *Relative points of view: linguistic representations of culture.* Oxford, Berghahn.

Whorf, B. L., Carroll, J. B. (1974). *Language, thought and reality: selected writings of Benjamin Lee Whorf.* Cambridge (Mass.), M.I.T.P.

Wickens, P. (1987). *The road to Nissan: flexibility, quality, teamwork.* London, Macmillan.

ON OTHERNESS

Where are you from? The importance of the located self[26]

Peter Cummins

> *Not only do most Psychologists refuse to take national identity seriously as a legitimate problem for research, those who do write on the problem seem bent on explaining it away in the course of preparing their moral case for universalistic utopianism* (Scheibe, 1998).

This quote identifies the central concern of this chapter. What happens if I did take the problem of (my) national identity seriously? Just what is the importance of national identity and what are the effects of living within a different national identity over a long period of time. Linked to this is the experience of working and thinking within a particular psychological framework (Personal Construct Psychology [PCP]; Kelly, 1991) over 20 years. While I am not aware that there is anything directly written within Kelly's work about this topic as ever I found that there are clues within PCP as to how we might go about understanding national identity:

> *Each man contemplates in his own personal way the stream of events upon which he finds himself so swiftly borne* (Kelly, 1991).

This chapter is my own contemplation about the stream of events which has led to me being invited to contribute to this book. In writing it there are three main questions to which I shall return more than once.

Who you are is a function of:

1. *Where* you are (?)
2. where you *have been* (?)
3. where you *hope to arrive* (?) (Benson, 2001).

To do this I use three main sources; the work of George Kelly, of Ciaran Benson and of Karl Scheibe. Kelly's Personal Construct Psychology has influenced my entire career as a clinical psychologist. Benson and Scheibe are much more recent discoveries who have both been of great help in clarifying what was bothering me and in assisting me to reconstrue this bother. Benson's work gave me a central clue as to how I would go about the task of

---

[26] This paper was originally published in German as: Cummins, P. (2001). Wo kommst du her? - Die Bedeutung des verorteten Selbst. in: J. Scheer (Ed.) (2001). *Identität in der Gesellschaft*. Giessen: Psychosozial-Verlag (26-37).

reconstruing - in particular his use of the concept of THE OTHER in relation to national Identity. Scheibe's work filled in a major gap in my knowledge of what has been written about the idea of self and where selfhood is derived from.

Cultural Psychology

In his book '*The Cultural Psychology of Self*' (Benson, 2001), Benson states that Cultural Psychology acknowledges explicitly:

- How one is located in one's community,
- how that community is located in its wider society,
- how that society stands in relation to other societies,
- how these relationships are placed developmentally and currently in history.

All have a profound relevance for the kinds of mind and self that may be formed.

Cultural psychology: examines how people make meaningful the world they find, make meaningful worlds and in the course of doing all these things construct themselves as types of person and self who inhabit these worlds (Benson, 2001).

Benson quotes Bruner:

The dominant questions for a cultural psychology of self have to do with the making and negotiation of meaning, with the construction of self and a sense of agency, with the acquisition of symbolic skills and with the cultural situatedness of all mental activity.

I want here to make an attempt using PCP to develop this idea of a cultural psychology of Myself, using the broad invitation provided by Jörn. The cultural psychology of a subject is, of course, an area, which he has worked on himself most notably in his paper for the Townsville PCP conference '"Congress language", Personal Constructs and Constructive Internationalism' (1996[27]). In this paper Jörn says, "I apologise that I am going to touch upon a number of topics that transcend my professional competence. In some instances, therefore, what I have to say is more based on personal convictions or experience that on the solid ground of scientific knowledge."

This is a disclaimer of which I would like to take full advantage!

Jörn focuses on the importance of different languages and the problems of translation and the difficulties of mutual understanding. I want to widen this

---

[27] Reprinted in this volume, p. 104-121 *(Ed.)*

discussion from language to place: *Who* I am and the language I speak is determined largely by *where I am located*. My very sense of self is moulded by the culture in which I develop. We can often have a real sense of where a person comes from by the sort of person they appear to be; "from his behaviour I do not think that he comes from here". As Benson puts it, "Self is a locative system".

Self, acts of self-location and locations are inextricably linked and mutually constructive leads to the importance of the cultural psychology of self. The key issue for Benson is the significance for himself of the ways and means by which he locates himself and is enabled to do so biologically and culturally which, taken together, constitute a fundamental part of his psychology. For Benson *the concept of self lies at the heart of this psychology of location* (my emphasis).

I have already described how I ended up living in England, in a paper which was the direct result of an invitation from Jörn (Cummins, 2000[28]). This paper has also been prompted by a similar direct invitation from Jörn. As already mentioned I was particularly interested in Jörn's paper on conference language (Scheer, 1996). He makes just one allusion to the differences between English speakers: "Other people, in this case British, complained that they did not understand some of the Australians, many of the Americans and so on" - but does not take this up, except to see it as a parallel to the difficulties experienced by speakers of other languages. As I thought about it I realised that what Jörn is hinting at here, that British people may not be able to understand Australians and Americans, can be attributed to two main causes, accent and different vocabularies. Both of these are usually part of what Scheibe (1998) calls our birthright: "That which one is, prior to the enactment of any achieved roles, is a result of the birthright". We are born within an ascribed sex, kinship, race and sometimes religion. The accent and vocabulary we develop is usually intimately bound up with our birthright.

We can of course try to alter both - a recent programme on British television attempted to teach a working class woman from the north of England to be able to pretend to be an upper class 'Lady XXX'. A major part of the month make over was to try to teach her to radically alter her accent; it is not just language that defines a person - within the same language system it is accent that determines much of how an individual is construed. At the end of the month the programme makers had to accept failure and alter their script, as they had not been able to sufficiently alter her accent. Clothes, mannerisms and life stories were much easier to alter than accent. I realised that accent is crucially about location and kinship. In most parts of the British Isles a strong

---

[28] Reprinted in this volume, p. 45-59 *(Ed.)*

regional accent has been seen as a statement of working class origins. Education often saw as one of its tasks to smooth out the regional accent. But this accent is the most powerful statement about where a person began their life. It usually also has a profound effect on how the person is construed by the OTHER.

"A person may for example, be firmly convinced that people with a certain kind of speech accent are ignorant and basely motivated" (Kelly, 1991). This is certainly one of the strong English stereotypes about anyone with a distinct Irish accent. Once they begin to speak such a person has begun to make a statement about where they come from: it is not just language that defines a person - within the same language system it is accent that determines much of how an individual is construed. As my central questions state: *Who* you are is a function of *where* you are, of where you *have been*, and of where you *hope to arrive*.

We cannot even begin to answer these without making some statement about the birthright we began with. One of the questions I have struggled with is to what extent it is possible to leave behind my birthright. I lived in Ireland for a total of 22 years; I have lived in England and Scotland for a total of 28 years. I do not think however that I will ever stop seeing myself as Irish. But what kind of Irish? (In Coventry the second generation Irish are known as 'Plastic Paddies', i.e. an inferior version of the real thing). In PCP terms I suspect that I have constructed a set of fragmented selves, where a fragmented self is defined as a set of incompatible subsystems. I have the self that is "pure Irish", the self that is anglicised and the self that attempts to integrate the previous two. The question is of course what is the cost of this fragmentation.

A recent discovery of Tom Ravenette's model of boundaries (in Fisher & Cornelius, 2001) helped to clarify this question. Ravenette's model utilises two constructs: *legitimate* vs *illegitimate*; and *Safety* vs *Danger*.

If we put these in a matrix we get

legitimate

Safety   Danger

illegitimate

In adopting an identity I can choose to try and 'become English'. This would be *illegitimate* but *safe* (as long as I am not discovered!). To proudly assert my Irish identity is *legitimate* but *dangerous* (the risk of rejection). I could decide to live solely within an Irish community (which would be seen by the host community as *illegitimate* but *safe*) and finally I can refuse to be anything but totally Irish in the wider community (*illegitimate* and *dange-*

rous). Ravenette's model helped me to see that there is no one adequate answer to the dilemma.

> *The Educated Person quite often succeeds in gaining liberation from the primitive emotional bonds into which he was accidentally born - but what is the psychological sequelae to this liberation?* (Scheibe, 1998)

Jörn's invitation has given me the opportunity to develop something which has been part of my life since I first came to England in 1973 - i.e. the sense that I lived among THE OTHER.

Where am I from

> *A fundamental problem confronting every one of us, and indeed every sentient creature, is how to position ourselves in the worlds we inhabit and how to find our way around them... Location is a basic ontological category for Psychology* (Benson, 2001).

In Bensons book 'The Cultural Psychology of Self' I found some of what I had been looking for. Location is a basic ontological category for psychology - this may be true, it certainly was no part of any psychology I have ever studied. And yet it makes so much intrinsic sense to me. I still struggle with the typical conference question 'Where are you from?' This can have several answers:

1.   I am from 'PCP Education and Training' (a training organisation)
2.   I am from Coventry Psychology service (my work place)
3.   I am from Near Rugby (where I live)
4.   I am from Dublin (where I came from)

Each of us lives in a complex set of interrelationships - being judged by a multiplicity of social judges. I can be judged as

-   How Irish am I,
-   How good a psychologist am I,
-   How good a parent am I,
-   How good a conference participant.

Much of the time the questioner actually is interested in the answer to 4 - it is my accent which has puzzled them. Living in a different English speaking society it is accent which acts as the differentiator of location. To alter ones accent can have a significant effect of how a person is seen. I discussed this recently with a Scottish friend: To my ears she has a distinct Scottish accent, yet in a recent telephone conversation to Scotland she was told "don't you sound English". I have had similar experiences while in Ireland - being told in Ireland that I sound English and in England being heard as Irish can lead to a sense of living in the in-between.

The starting point of every journey is here ... The point of reference for each and every moment of the journey is here and its conclusion is when the there of destination becomes the here of arrival. (Benson, op. cit.)

This can be linked to the journey of emigration - when I stop thinking of Ireland as the reference point and realise that England has become *here*, e.g. when talking to my children while in Ireland, England is home for them and by implication me, so I find myself hesitating over the use of the language "when we get home". In the act of doing so I am acknowledging that move- ment *from there to here*.

As Kelly points out, the degree to which we can relate to the other depends on how well we understand that other persons view of the world. Being mis- construed in both countries makes social understanding a difficult venture!

The more interested I got in this the more I became aware of the large litera- ture on self-studies. I am no expert in this field. The book, which I became aware of through a personal communication from Du_an Stojnov, was *'Self studies; the psychology of self and identity'* (Scheibe, 1998).

Where did my self come from

Scheibe makes the interesting distinction between:

Degradation of social role - Advancement.

By degradation of social role he means roles that are seen as inferior e.g. convicts, psychiatric patients. Advancement refers to roles which give high status e.g. medals, job promotion. Using this concept we can see that it is possible to be Irish in England - *degraded social role* - and at the same time be *advanced* by being a consultant clinical psychologist. This framework has allowed me to make sense of a clinical reality - that of patients making dispa- raging remarks about the Irish (knowing that I was Irish) while still according me the respect of a professional whom they saw as providing the therapy they needed. As Scheibe points out, a person's social identity at any time is a function of his or her validated social positions. This means that we are con- stantly faced with the necessity of locating ourselves in relation to others. This location is psychological in the sense that Scheibe is referring to but directly physical in the sense that Benson is referring to.

As Benson goes on to point out: "The fact of being located is central to the concept of selfhood".

But where am I located - what does it mean to be located? For some people there is a definite denial of any such linkage. The Spanish artist Jean Munozis is quoted in the *Observer* (a British Sunday newspaper) as saying when asked if he felt like a Spanish artist: "I never feel that you are bound by your territory...I don't work with anyone in Spain...When I am here (in Madrid) I am in my studio. *I am an exile at home* (my emphasis)". This, remember, is a Spaniard talking about living in Spain. I start from a different perspective but one that still leaves me as an exile at home (*Being Irish living in England*).

'Nothing can be without being in place' (Aristotle)

My early interest in PCP came from Kelly's definition of guilt. Having been brought up in a standard Irish Catholicism I was an expert in being guilty. The church of my childhood was very keen on getting people to understand their guilt, which begins at birth with the doctrine of original sin. The newborn is lucky to be given the gifts of the church to expiate this guilt and strive for a better life. Kelly's emphasis on the importance of one's core role gave me the way of understanding my guilt and of being able to reconstrue it without the church provided methods. In the early 1980's I spent an afternoon with an English Benedictine monk. We discussed my thoughts about Christianity and Catholicism in particular. Towards the middle of the afternoon he said to me: "Peter, you are a typical Irish catholic of the 50's; we are not like that any more". I was very struck by this comment - I was typical of a time and a place. What did it mean to be Irish and a catholic - particularly as I have now lived in England for longer than I ever lived in Ireland.

The history of being Irish in Britain has been changing rapidly in the time I have lived in Scotland and then England. Just before my time it was not unknown to see signs *'Room for rent - no Irish or coloureds'*. I was fascinated to see Scheibe (1998) use a similar example: "Not only does the nature of the birthright grant determine the respect in which a person is initially held (and in turn the self respect that it generates) but it also determines the possibilities for the individual to gain access to attained positions within the society because of linkages that are explicitly or implicitly codified within a society to regulate the promotion process". Thus the rule *'No Irish need apply'* constitutes a barrier to promotion resulting from the particular character of a granted component of identity.

The typical stereotype of the Irish was of stupid people who worked in manual jobs. This image has had a long history, going back to Irish labourers who dug the canal system and probably before that (I am no historian). In more recent times the stereotype of the Irish as all literary gifted people has developed, fuelled by an increase in the profile of Irish writers and Poets. But

I think my favourite stereotype was one I read in a Sunday paper: "Being Irish, he is of course good with horses!!"

Benson suggests that "the other is that in dialogue with which I define my own identity. I think of myself as being that which the other is not and each we does the same ... *England has been Ireland's great other*" (my emphasis). This phrase was a real revelation for me. I referred earlier to a feeling of the sense that "I lived among the OTHER". I also have been fascinated by a psychology, which is a psychology of the other (PCP). At the heart of PCP is the insight that we cannot understand anything without having some sense of its contrast pole. "A construct is a way in which some things are construed as being alike and yet different from others " (Kelly, 1991).

Inevitably I have been living out this by living in England. Who I am is a function of where I am i.e. where I am can define my sense of which OTHER I am using to define myself. Travelling in the US I often met people who were delighted to hear that I am Irish. I too am Irish, they announced. As it turned out they usually had Irish ancestry 5 or more generations back - rarely if ever had they been to Ireland. I was very aware that I did not see them as Irish - I construed them as American. This was in contrast to experiencing myself as European for the first time and realising that I had more in common with a German speaker than I had with an English speaking American (in PCP terms, European identity was superordinate to common language).

Again a framework provided by Scheibe provides the interesting construct:

ascribed (granted or given)   vs   *attained* (elected)

While Irish Americans would see their identity as *ascribed* I was seeing it as *attained*, i.e. they had chosen to develop this identity on the basis of very distant ancestral roots. I suppose I saw them as having some choice they could see themselves as *American* or *Irish American* whereas I had no choice - I was born Irish. There is of course some room for argument here - most famously the Duke of Wellington who was born in Dublin: When he was called Irish he replied *"because a man is born in a stable does that make him a horse"*. It follows from this comment that it is possible to move from *granted* national identity to *attained*. I wonder how true this is - I myself do not think it would be easy to become another nationality; while I could acquire another passport I could never stop thinking of myself as Irish. However I do think that after living in a different culture for a long time you inevitably acquire many of the traits of the dominant culture. I have some sense of how English have I become - not used to spending time talking to shopkeepers; expect people to be punctual; suspicious when someone starts talking at a bus stop; unwillingness to humour people; expect people to do what they have said they will (as contrasted with a common Irish unwillingness to offend people so avoid giving offence by evasion rather than confrontation of problem area).

> *The culturally distinctive features of a people are the ways in which their interpretations of the world channel how they act in it. This sense of themselves as a distinct people is part of the foundation for what is called national identity* (Benson, 2001).

It is clear that others have found it possible to do what I have found difficult to contemplate, i.e. to change nationality. While writing this chapter an Obituary appeared in the Times newspaper of an ex member of the IRA. The opening sentence of this obituary observes:

> *More than one Englishman has become so enchanted with the Emerald Isle (Ireland) that he has invented a whole new persona for himself ... none went quite as far ... as an East London boy called John Stephenson who turned himself into Sean MacStiofain ... brought up in London he was told by his mother just before she died (when he was seven): "I'm Irish, therefore you are Irish ... don't forget it".*

"I never did" MacStiofain later said. He spent the rest of his life involved in the Irish republican movement learning to speak Irish and moving to Ireland. (the majority of people in Ireland cannot speak the Irish language) ... In his own view he clearly became Irish, derived from the *birthright* passed on to him by his mother. The obituary ends however by pointing out that

> *as it turned out his implacable sense of Irishness was - tragically or comically - a deluded one ... a journalist discovered that John Stephenson was one eight Irish at best ... although she claimed to be from Belfast his mother was born in London with just one Irish grandmother.*

It is very clear here that the writer sees MacStiofain as having been deluded because of the lack of an inherited birthright ... no constructivist there! He could not be Irish despite a lifetime lived as such because his mother had not got a full Irish ancestry. But his mother for whatever reason clearly construed herself as Irish and passed this on to her son.

It is clear from MacStiofain's own description that his was a very emotionally driven decision, linked to his mother's dying wish. He would appear to have successfully changed his own national identity by adopting what he was told was his birthright.

As I described earlier the core of this chapter is the idea that *who* you are is a function of

- *where* you are,

- of where you *have been*
- and of where you *hope to arrive.*

I conclude that I am someone who is a long term English resident who comes from Ireland. I now see that I need to arrive at an understanding of how two sets of OTHER can be integrated into a meaningful structure that can help me to say where do I come from and to end up with a clearer sense of where I hope to arrive.

Where do I hope to arrive

In this chapter I have begun to understand why Jörn's work has intrigued me - the sense of a language self he has identified is extended to a sense of place and accent linked to that place. It fits well within this book as Jörn has (perhaps unwittingly) been a major stimulus in my development of this theme. This is in turn extended using Scheibe's key ideas of *ascribed* vs. *attained* and *degraded social role* vs. *advancement*. The idea of a personal cultural idea of self helps to coalesce ideas, which I have lacked the structure to explore. Benson's central idea of the OTHER (and national Identity) links into PCP and begins to clarify why it makes such intrinsic sense to me. As previously stated PCP is a psychology of THE OTHER. Inevitably PCP itself has to be seen as a psychology of Kelly's own cultural self. "Kelly's pioneering background - he and his parents were literally among the last 'homesteaders' on the American frontier - undoubtedly predisposed him to conceptualise human behavior in terms of an exploration or quest" (Neimeyer, 1985).

This chapter has been an attempt to clarify part of my own exploration. In doing so I have been very aware that the question of national and personal identity is one that can become highly politically charged (particularly in the context of English/Irish identities!). But this risk is probably a useful emotional indicator of using PCP to properly advance understanding. When Kelly was asked what area he would most like to see PCP being developed he replied "Politics" (Fransella, 2001). In a very small-scale personal way I hope that this chapter has been a personal political extension of the value of PCP. For this is where I hope to arrive - at an understanding of the meaning of living within a different national identity and my struggle to arrive at an integrated sense of where I have been; of where I am and of where I hope to arrive.

References

Benson, C. (2001). *The cultural psychology of self.* London: Routledge.

Cummins, P. (2000). Snakes in Ireland. In Scheer J. (Ed.). *The Person in society, challenges to a constructivist theory.* Giessen: Psychosozial-Verlag.

Fransella, F. (2000). Perspectives: past, present and future. In Fisher J.M., Cornelius N. (Eds.). *Challenging the boundaries - PCP perspectives for the new millennium.* Farnborough: EPCA publications.

Kelly, G.A. (1991). *The psychology of personal constructs.* London: Routledge.

Neimeyer, R.A. (1985). *The development of personal construct psychology.* Lincoln/London: University of Nebraska Press.

Ravenette, T. (2000). Preface of: Fisher J.M., Cornelius N. (Eds). *Challenging the boundaries - pcp perspectives for the new millennium.* Farnborough: EPCA publications.

Scheer, J. W. (1996). "Congress" language, personal constructs, and constructive internationalism. In Walker B. et. al. (Eds.). *Personal construct theory, a psychology for the future*; APS.

Scheibe, K.E. (1998). *Self studies, the psychology of self and identity*; Connecticut: Praeger.

A psychology of immigrants interacting with members of established culture groups

James C. Mancuso

Theoretical propositions

A venturer whose surname ends in a vowel, who had passed through primary schools, in The USA, during the decade of the 1930s, and who had spent 30 years as a professor promulgating personal construct theory would have had the opportunity to author thousands of narratives about interactions between self and other.

The formulation of the perspective developed in this essay relies heavily on the dichotomy corollary of George Kelly's (1991/1955) theory of personal constructs: "… a person's construction system is composed of a finite number of dichotomous constructs" (p. 41). That reliance is based, in part, on a confidence that the corollaries associated with Kelly's theory have gained support from a long chain of scholarship (Fransella, 2003), and that personal construct theory can guide the formulation of a perspective that can usefully frame the interactions of members of different cultures who occupy the same geographical space.

The development of this essay elaborates the dichotomy corollary by specifying the assumption that persons use superordinate dichotomous constructs that subordinate a congeries of dichotomous constructs. Using other terms, a theorist might say: "A person assigns an object or event to a category on the basis of detecting and then matching the attributes (properties, features[29]) of an object or an event to the attributes of a prototypical member of a category." However, a constructivist construes 'categorization processes' in terms of a person having located an object or event on a series of constructs and then inductively determining that the object or event can be construed by use of the superordinating, complex construct. For example, in order to locate

---

[29] In this essay, I avoid the use of terms such as *features, attributes,* and *properties.* Using those terms can prompt the inference that a person 'detects characteristics' in objects or events. I intend that a reader should focus on a person's assigning attributes by locating events on personal two-poled constructs.

a person on the sad end of a personal *sad/happy* superordinate construct the construing person must first determine that the target person can be located at the left hand pole of subordinated personal constructs such as *frowning/smiling*, *lethargic/animated*, and so on.

Another of this essay's foundational premises derives directly from Kelly's fundamental postulate "… a person's processes are psychologically channelized by the ways in which he anticipates events" (Kelly, 1991/1955, p. 32).

Theorists (Mancuso, 1996, Mancuso & Sarbin, 1983) have adduced support for elaborating Kelly's fundamental postulate by assuming that anticipation involves the constant creation of self-guiding narratives. Each element of a narrative results from a millisecond-by-millisecond building of psychollages through which one construes ('recognizes') the objects and events that provide the flow of sensory inputs to the person's sensory systems.

At this point, it would be useful to clarify how the term *psychollage* will be used in this essay. I (Mancuso, 2000) have recommended that theorists replace the traditional term *category* with the term *psychollage*. The term *psychollage* would signify a collage of meaning, a "something" that a personal construct psychologist might discuss in terms of locating an object or event at a specified location on a personal construct. A personal psychollage can be regarded as the end product of having located an object or event at a position on a bi-polar judgment construct, especially when the construct used is a complex, superordinate construct.

As a person builds self-guiding anticipatory narratives, he/she must create psychollages that define the role of all objects and events – including self – that will be involved in the narrative's enactment. For example, in an interaction with his or her social ecology a person may build a self-guiding narrative by using the psychollage that results from having located his her self on the sad end of his/her personal *sad/happy* superordinate construct. Thereupon, the person may build a self guiding narrative which specifies outcomes of his/her enactment of the role of a sad person.

Successful anticipation depends on the outcomes of the enactment of the self-guiding narrative matching the outcomes that had been set in the person's anticipatory narrative. Ultimately, each element of a self-guiding narrative must be construed in ways that will lead to successful anticipation of the outcome of the self-guiding narrative.

A person can construct a self-guiding narrative that will not lead to successful anticipation. In such instances, a human automatically prepares for action (See Mascolo & Mancuso, 1990). For example, a person might construe her self as a sad person as she builds an anticipatory narrative that specifies the anticipated outcome as her fiend offering a sympathetic response. The friend might, instead, berate the actor for succumbing to the pressures of her daily life. Physiological and anatomical functioning changes accompany such failures in anticipation; and those changes do affect sensory elements. Thereupon, the actor will 'feel' the results of the body changes. In contexts of failed anticipations, persons will probably construe the associated sensory inputs as one or another emotion, depending on the context in which the narrative is enacted (See Mancuso & Sarbin, 1998). The anatomical and physiological changes can aid adaptation, in that the changes do prepare a person for the effort involved in devising alternative psychollages that can be used to construct an alternative anticipatory narrative.

The complex *Self/Other* construct[30]

In the process of psychological development, a person learns to use the complex construct *self/other*. Self would be located on the right hand pole of constructs such as *external to my skin/internal to my skin,* and *controlled by outside elements/controlled by internal processes*. Other would be construed by locating a person on the left hand pole of such constructs.

The *other/self* construct would subordinate many superordinate constructs. The psychollage that would result from construing a particular object as self would require that the construer locate that object at one or the other pole a large set of superordinate constructs. A particular object that would be construed as other would have been located on the contrast poles of those superordinate constructs. The psychollage used to construe self would stand as a contrast to the psychollage that would be used to construe other. The psychollage *other*, like the psychollage *self*, results from accessing and using a large set of superordinate constructs.

Creating psychollages to construe the other

As an example of building and using psychollages to construe the other, I present Kate Weatheral, who can readily access a psychollage to which she could attach the label *Italian-American*[31]. The left-hand pole of her complex

---

[30] The extent of effort to formulate a useful perspective on the ways in which a person develops the construct other/self can be assessed by reviewing the bibliographies on self-related topics that one can access at the www address http://www2.canisius.edu/~gallaghr/pibib.html#index. The position on which the text of this essay is based is elaborated in the work of Mancuso & Ceely (1980), Mancuso & Sarbin (1983) and Mancuso (1996).

[31] Throughout this essay, I will make frequent reference to psychollages used to construe Italian-Americans. I assume, however, that one can generalize many of my observations and conclusions to situations involving other people who immigrate to a

153

construct *Italian-Americans/we* would be superordinate to and aligned with the left hand poles of a series of subordinate constructs. In turn, the left hand pole of Kate's *Italian-Americans/we* construct would be aligned with the left hand pole of her superordinate *they/we* construct. Whenever Kate encountered a person whom she could locate on certain easily-used constructs so that she could assign attributes to that person – *vowel-ending name, dark hair, olive tinted skin, dark eyes, thick and arched eyelashes* – she can immediately access her personal categorizing psychollage *Italian-American*. Meeting Josephine Conti, for example, Kate can construe Josephine using the personal psychollage by which she could 'know' – construe – Italian-Americans. By doing so – using a psychological process that everyone uses as he/she attempts to anticipate the continued flow of inputs – she could make inferences that would prompt her to assign other attributes to Josephine. In other language, Kate had followed out implicative relations in her hierarchically arranged system of two-poled constructs and had assigned, without direct confirmatory evidence, other attributes to Josephine – *poor table manners, excessive emotionality, limited sophistication, lawless*, and *so forth*.

When Kate Weatheral uses her *they/we* superordinate construct, which is superordinate to her *Italian-American/we* construct, she cannot have determined which constructs are subordinate to the *Italian-American/we* construct through personal experience. While attending schools and colleges largely populated by people who shared her upper-socioeconomic, old New England family heritage, she has had very little contact with descendants of the Italy-to-The-USA immigration. After her marriage, she had no opportunity to associate with Italian-Americans as she participated in the social and civic activities opened to her by her family's status in her community. She had not read carefully researched anthropological studies of the people of Southern Italy and Sicily – the region from which most of the Italy-to-The-USA immigrants had originated.

Like most citizens of The USA, Kate had been exposed to some of the countless media and literary productions that portray Italian-Americans as primitive, lawless, and over passionate consumers of mounds of tomato based, olive-oil laden foods. Each such exposure implicitly demonstrated to her that 'they' used construct systems that differed from her personal construct system. That is, each of her contacts with the other has created a condition that would prompt her to consider the possibility that the psychollages that she could generate from her construct system would not represent 'accurate' images of 'out there reality'. Perhaps, for example, the portrayals of the intense family-centered social activity of Italian-Americans would clearly indicate that 'they' located such activity at the good end of their *bad/good* super-

---

geographic space already occupied by adherents to a well-established culture.

ordinate construct. If so, would that suggest to Kate that they would construe the rather aloof, cool relationships among her family members as bad?

Kate's discomfort over having her construings of family life invalidated by others – specifically, Italian-Americans – might have been relieved had she participated in a sociology course through which she would have been introduced to some of the sociologists' writings about Southern Italians and the communities of Italian-American immigrants (for example, Banfield, 1958; Gans, 1982). Banfield's treatise, for example, would have prompted her to assign the traits of *anarchic, self-centeredness, suspiciousness, conservativism, vanity,* and *ignorance* to people who were reared in a Southern Italian/Sicilian culture. And, Kate would have been induced to believe, that those traits, according to Banfield, were associated with 'amoral familism': a form of 'bad' family life.

The creation of and utility of stereotypes

The kind of analysis incorporated into Banfield's 1958 monograph came from a long tradition of 'discovering' and attributing special personality characteristics to 'races' and cultural groups. Trait theories assumed special credibility when persons esteemed as scientists promulgated propositions about genetic[32] transmission of personality characteristics. Social considerations prompted ready acceptance of such theories. For example, genetic theories could frame the social problems created during the decades following the year 1880, during which time emigration from Italy eventually settled about 4 million 'Others' in The USA. The people who had settled in The USA prior to that population movement could easily detect the differences between their own favored ideologies and psychollages and those that guided the conduct of the mass of Italian immigrants (Mangione & Morreale, 1992, pp. 214-237).

Among other cultural practices, those immigrants imported a version of the Roman Catholic religion that differed from the version practiced by the parishioners of the Roman Catholic churches that had been established by the Irish immigrants (Orsi, 1985). The dietary habits of the Italian-Americans, particularly the emphasis on the use of unfamiliar vegetables, an emphasis on plant products as a source of protein, and use of olive oil, contrasted sharply to the dietary habits of people who had imported the northern and western European cultures to The USA. The rigidly enforced moral standards develo-

---

[32] To read a summary survey of the ways in which some of the most respected social scientists of the era thought about issues related to eugenics, one can access the material found on the WWW at the address: http://www.mugu.com/galton/essays/1900-1911/galton-1904-am-journ-soc-eugenics-scope-aims.htm.

ped in small villages that were based on agricultural economies differed notably from the moral standards that were acceptable to the established urban population of the cities in which the immigrants settled. The immigrants continued to practice modes of establishing families and the maintaining of loyalties to the extended family and family networking structures. Those practices were overtly buttressed by the use of honorific titles and rituals that had been developed over centuries of life in villages in which the family represented the major source of social support. The immigrants continued to follow their frugal economic practices in a country in which they had access to an abundance that was unknown in a country of their origin. The styles of dress and personal grooming of many of the immigrants easily allowed the established peoples to identify them as Italian immigrants.

Following the psychological formulations outlined in the earlier section of this essay, one may advance the proposition that these cultural differences would provide immediate contrasts and invalidation of the psychollages embedded in the narratives that customarily guided the conduct of the majority of the already established inhabitants of The USA. The reactions of the members of the established populations might be expressed crudely by statements such as, 'Why don't those dagoes do things the way we do them? Why don't they see things the way we do?' Confronting the possibility that 'the ways that we see things' might be questioned, the members of the established inhabitants could be prompted to agree that there was a need to engage in a process of eliminating that possible sources of invalidation.

The established inhabitants could reduce instances of invalidation and could support their own ideologies and psychollages by regarding as inferior the ideologies and psychollages generated and supported by Southern Italian culture. The religious practices of the Italian immigrants could be seen as primitive remnants of Roman paganism. The foodstuffs consumed by the immigrants could be perceived as greasy animal fare. The reliance on close knit family and friendship structures could be construed as a remnant of the Roman client system that was antithetical to the community-oriented social structures that promoted participatory democracy. Furthermore, the family structures enhanced the possibilities of carrying on secretive, perhaps illegal, behaviors. The frugality of the immigrants, particularly when the funds accumulated through the practice of frugality were sent back to families in Italy, could be construed as unpatriotic and subversive.

The literate established inhabitants of The USA who wished to adopt the tactic of denigrating the Southern Italian and Sicilian culture could readily find a widely disseminated psychollage for use in construing members of that culture. The central government of the Italian state that had been established in 1870 had encountered serious problems as they had attempted to govern the people of the section of south Italy once known as the Kingdom of The

Two Sicilies. Many inhabitants of the subjugated kingdom remained sympathetic to the deposed Bourbon monarchy, its nobility, and the princes of the church who had been an integral part of the Bourbon power structure. Laboring and peasant class people had no voting rights, but were subject to military conscription. Banditry, often indistinguishable from terrorist and revolutionary guerilla activity, flourished throughout Southern Italy. A young man who could not manage to emigrate could choose to join a bandit corps rather than await conscription into an army destined for duty in one of Italy's misguided African campaigns.

Leaders of the new state took recourse to outright military occupation in order to bring about the creation of the unified state that they had anticipated. Political and military leaders, helped by commentators and literary figures, could access genetic theories to create and then use the superordinate construct *Southern Italian/ideal Italian*. That construct subordinated the constructs *ungovernable/law-abiding, primitive/sophisticated,* and *over passionate/reasonable* (See Schneider, 1998; Dickie, 1999). By use of that stereotype (a categorizing psychollage used indiscriminately to construe members of a putative group of persons) a prime minister, for example, could explain to other European leaders the necessity of using the kinds of repression that allowed the arrest and incarceration of families of suspected brigands and the summary military trial and execution of death penalties on captured brigands.

During the decades in which large numbers of Italians immigrated into the USA, the productions of esteemed scholars (Goddard, 1912; Davenport, 1911), who were supported by some of the most powerful figures in The USA (See Kevles, 1985), had advanced acceptance of theories that associated personality characteristics with genetic function. Those theories lent credibility to the formulation of descriptions of 'racial' types. The elite segment of the population of The USA – whose scions attended high prestige universities where professors advocated eugenics theories – could construe the Southern Italian immigrants as carriers of genes associated with negative characteristics. That application of genetic theories of inherited characteristics acquired special credibility following the dissemination of the works of the Cesare Lombroso[33]; an Italian physician/criminologist who had gained fame as a scholar who had applied eugenics language to discuss crime and the unwanted behaviors of Southern Italians.

The general public could, as well, acquire the stereotypes of Southern Italians through exposure to the popular media of information. The world-wide dis-

---

[33] See Gibson (2002) for an analysis of the profound effects of Lombroso's work.

tribution of media that has produced a feast of variations on the stereotype (See D'Acierno, 1999; Italic Studies Institute, 2002) has allowed people who might never interact with an Italian-American to use the stereotype to construe anyone who can be regarded as an Italian-American. The study reported by the Italian Studies Institute (2002) analyzed 1233 films depicting Italian and Italian-Americans. In those films, produced during the period between 1928 and 2002, 859 films (69 per cent) portrayed Italians in a negative light. Forty per cent of the films (500) portrayed Italians as mobsters: most of whom (88 per cent) were fictional characters. Another 359 (29 per cent) films portrayed Italians as boors, bimbos, or buffoons.

Eliminating the source of invalidations in self/other interactions

When using the assumptions described in the first section of this essay, an analyst would expect that Kate Weatheral would experience an arousal reaction when she observes real life and media presentations of immigrants using psychollages that would differ from the psychollages that she and her validating community would build out of their personal construct systems. Rather than construing the arousal as an emotion labeled simply *arousal*, she would find social support for interpreting her arousal reaction as *anger*, or *displeasure* or *disgust*. In that way, she would spare herself the psychological problems of regarding the practices of the members of the alien culture as an invalidation of the universal adequacy of the construct systems that guide the members of her culture. For example, she might observe members of an Italian-American family bidding good-by to another member of the family. Their weeping, hugging, and kissing would reflect their use of a construct system that would differ considerably from the construct system used by her family members. Kate would have little reason to associate her experience of her arousal reaction with an invalidation. More likely, had she absorbed the naive psychological theory that one absorbs in cultures in which such arousal reactions are construed as discrete emotions, Kate would readily attribute her arousal to disgust generated a by display of a 'characteristic' of excess passion.

Such 'disgust' prompted one group of influential persons to propose a curtailment of the immigration of cultural groups whose behavior would belie the universal validity of preferred psychollages (preferred ways of 'seeing' objects and events). Other influential persons – those who understood the necessity of importing inexpensive labor to provide needed low-cost person power – could promote the use of a socially created psychollage designated by the term *assimilation*.

Limiting immigration

The efforts of the anti-immigration coterie resulted in the convoluted immigration laws that took effect, in The USA, in 1924. By basing the quotas of immigrants allowed into The USA on the census of 1890, the laws granted special privilege to immigrants from the Northern and Western European countries – countries assumed to be inhabited by 'genetically and culturally superior' people. The enforcement of these quota systems effected a decrease in the numbers of immigrants who carried cultures that prompted the use of construct systems that differed from those of power holders of the established USA population.

Prompting 'assimilation'

Social scientists and educators offered another means of avoiding such disgust. They tried to describe a process that could be signified by the term *assimilation*. Ellwood Cubberly, the first dean of Stanford University's School of Education, earned high status by producing text such as the following:

> Our task is to break up these groups of settlements, to assimilate and amalgamate these people [Southern and Eastern Europeans] as part of our American race, and to implant in their children as far as can be done, the Anglo-Saxon conception of righteousness, law and order, and popular government ... (Cubberly, 1909, p. 15, material in brakkets inserted by JCM).

Social workers also demonstrated their faith in the positive outcomes of promoting assimilation by founding settlement houses (Addams, 1912[34]), which served the purpose of inducing immigrants to become members of a cosmopolitan American society (Lissak, 1989). Social scientists served by doing studies that tracked the levels of success of the assimilation process (See Salins, 1997).

The most esteemed social scientists who initially propounded the use of the assimilation psychollage defined the process in terms of the then-prevailing behaviorist theories[35]. According to behaviorist formulations, proper dispensation of reward would prompt aliens[36] to express overtly those behaviors

---

[34] The text of this book is available on the WWW at the address:
http://digital.library.upenn.edu/women/addams/hullhouse/hullhouse.html

[35] E. L. Thorndike, who is regarded as a pioneer in the promotion of behaviorist theories, also promoted propositions supporting eugenic formulations.

[36] I use the term alien, intending to signify the construction that would be evoked by the Latin root of that term – *other*.

that would confirm the superiority of the behaviors of the members of the dominant society. Conversely, punishments would lead to the suppression of overt behaviors that belied the superiority of the behaviors endorsed by members of the dominant society. In consequence, assimilationists gave little thought to the ideologies and construct systems that underlay the behavior of the aliens. A behaviorist would have no reason to regard behavior in terms of self-defining psychollages built from a construct system acquired in a person's primary culture. So long as the alien did not behave in ways that offered invalidation to members of the dominant society, there would be no need to prompt change. In other terms, so long as the alien adopted behaviors that could indicate that he regarded the construction system of members of the dominant culture to be valid, he could be 'assimilated' into the broader society and could earn the 'goodies' that members of that society could dispense.

The puzzles that the alien would need to solve when considering that he/she would be subjected to the programs devised by the assimilationists would be framed by the general question: 'How much of the construct system of the dominant culture must I absorb before I will be absorbed into the dominant culture?' The venturer[37] was never presented with a list of the constructs and psychollages whose use would allow him/her access to 'positive reinforcers'.

During the period that the assimilationists held hegemony over many of the public education systems in the United States, a child of the Italian immigrants could frequently enter situations in which his/her enactment of behaviors guided by his/her anticipatory narratives would lead to unexpected outcomes. A behaviorist might easily construe those negative outcomes as negative reinforcers that would suppress enactment of unwanted behaviors. If for example, the venturing child believed that there was an advantage to speaking the language, other than English, that he/she might have learned in his/her home, his/her teachers could readily invalidate that belief by recourse to a variety of techniques. On hearing two children using terms from an Italian dialect in a conversation, a teacher might say, "We live in The USA, not in Italy. We speak English here in America." Or, the teacher could show his/her sophistication by denigrating the use of dialect rather than 'proper' Italian.

Defining self in an assimilationist ambience

D'Acierno (1999), as he proceeds through his analysis of stereotype creation through popular cinema, asks:

---

[37] I use the term *venturer* to designate an alien who attempts to interact effectively with members of a dominant culture.

What is it about the Italian-American identity and the cultural experi-
ence through which that identity has been formed that makes Italian
Americans so susceptible ... to the vicious underside of that process:
the internalization of, and the colonization by, the system of stereoty-
pes imposed by the dominant culture? (p. 619)

Cases of personal efforts to assimilate

Angelo Pellegrini and Henry Suzzallo – who shared a long tenure at University of Washington – illustrate clearly the varied ways in which even highly educated members have reacted to 'colonization' efforts (Mancuso & Rossellini, 2001).

In 1913, Angelo Pellegrini, aged 10 years, accompanied his mother and his four siblings on the 31-day journey from his small native village in Tuscany to McCleary, Washington, where his father had found steady employment in the lumber industry. Though he entered school in the USA with no knowledge of the English language, Pellegrini achieved high success in the education system of Washington State. Eventually he earned a doctor's degree and was appointed to a professorship at the University of Washington. When he was a young man, his self identity as a meliorator of the conditions of the marginalized, less powerful members of the society led him to join the communist party.

When he was forty-five years old, Pellegrini was called before a legislative committee that had set out to discover whether or not adherents of left wing movements were proselytizing among the impressionable students who attended the University of Washington. Fortunately, the committee was forced to disband before it could exercise its full power to add Pellegrini to a black list. Immediately after that threat to his career, Pellegrini (1986) enjoyed his most "productive decades" (p. 6) by attempting to achieve "happiness through self-realization" (p. 6). It was during those productive decades that he wrote one after another treatise on how one can achieve a satisfying self identity by construing his self as a perpetuator of many of the basic ideals of the Italian peasant culture as he knew it.

He summarized his position in the following text:

... Where the conditon to his well being are contingent [one] must act
as a citizen; but where they are purely a matter of his own will and
initiative, he must bestir himself as an individual ...

[In this book] I have emphasized activities and attitudes that seem to
me most frequently neglected sources of felicity. Implicit in the va-
rious anecdotes relating to the experience of the immigrant, and in all

161

the trivia about bread and wine, is the simple lesson that the home is the appropriate place where man may realize some part of his dignity.

... Resourcefulness and self-reliance in providing for the family's immediate needs are ancestral virtues which one should strive to rediscover. The pursuit of these ends will yield a measure of contentment of which no man should deprive himself. (Pellegrini, 1984/1948, pp. 230-231)

The results of Henry Suzzallo's quest contrast sharply to the results of Pellegrini's quest. Suzzallo assumed the post of president of University of Washington in 1914. His presidency ended when he was forced out of the position as a result of the actions of a lumber baron whom he apparently had alienated; and who, in the course of his conflict with Suzzallo, demeaningly referenced Suzzallo's origin in the Italian-American society.

On May 29, 1931, Henry Suzzallo who had left the presidency of University of Washington five years earlier gave a lecture to The Pilgrim's Society in London. Suzzallo informed his audience that his physical heritage included nothing from the Anglo-Saxon peoples. This son of an immigrant family averred, nevertheless, that everything in his thinking and aspirations had been obtained entirely from the Anglo-Saxon tradition as it was transmitted to him through the educational system of The United States! To speculate on the implications that might be drawn from this declaration, one must know that, Suzzallo studied at Columbia University's Teacher's College while on leave of absence from a position in Stanford University's School of Education. In 1905, Suzzallo earned a doctor's degree. In the same year, Edward Cubberly, Suzzallo's mentor, also completed his doctorate at Columbia.

Suzzallo did not leave a clear record of his having committed himself to assimilationist ideologies, as did Cubberly (see above citation). One must assume, however, that he found favor with the faculty of Teacher's College, several of whom promoted eugenics theories. Shortly after completing his doctor's degree and returning to Stanford University Suzzallo accepted a position as professor in Teacher's College. In that position he associated with other professor's who strongly endorsed eugenic positions. Nicholas M. Butler, the then-president of Columbia University expressed the esteem in which Suzzallo was held by recommending, in 1914, that University of Washington offer the position of president to Suzzallo.

In the course of having moved from the role of son in an immigrant family that operated a restaurant in San Jose, California, Henry Suzzallo was able to obliterate not only his baptismal name, Anthony, but also any ability to remember how his primary culture had influenced the development of the personal construct system that allowed him to achieve extraordinary academic and career success. He did not hesitate to display his belief that his having

162

done his best to adopt the construct system of the entrenched society's power holders had allowed him to enter the high places in the dominant society[38].

Accommodating to the construct systems of 'Others'

The foregoing text in this essay outlines a constructivist perspective on the psychological issues that come into magnified focus when a large number of aliens – 'others' – migrate into a geographical space that is already occupied by people who use a construct system that differs markedly from the system shared by large numbers of others. The core of the problematic issues is associated with the ensuing reciprocal invalidation. Whenever a person observes a person acting in ways that the observer would not act, the observer implicitly or explicitly assumes that one or another aspect of his/her construction system has been called into question – that one or another of his/her psychollages does not reflect 'reality' correctly.

Records of human history provide one after another example of the ways in which humans – especially humans who have acquired power – have sought to eliminate sources of such invalidation. Cain, according to the religious books of major religions, killed his brother, Abel. However one interprets the myth, it is safe to say that the chronicler meant to indicate that the very first humans developed the tactic of killing the source of invalidation. There is no shortage of chronicling of the number of humans who have been eliminated because they had acted as invalidators to persons who had access to the means of killing invalidators.

The Cain and Abel myth includes an example of another means of eliminating an invalidator. The deity, whose view of righteousness had been invalidated by Cain's conduct, sent Cain into exile. Through history, one finds many examples of how power centers have legalized prison colonies, prisons, and other forms of banishment to remove invalidators from their society.

Many societies, however, abrogated the use of death and banishment as means of eliminating sources of invalidation. Power centers, instead, advocated the use of 'educational' or 'reform' techniques.

During the 20th Century, social scientists and educators invented and crudely defined the education-related technique that would be signified by the term *assimilation*. The process, it was hypothesized, would succeed in eliminating the sources of invalidation that were carried into a country by immigrants

---

[38] One could associate the arousal experienced during his strenuous efforts to assimilate with the cardiac disorders that lead to Suzzallo's death at age 58. Pellegrini lived to age 88.

who used construct systems that differed from those used by the established population.

Despite the long-time efforts of the assimilationists, scholars (Salins, 1997, Christopher, 1988) continue to debate the matter of whether or not assimilation has or can solve the problem of eliminating invalidation. Advocates of assimilation have not been able to articulate clearly the articles of the contract that seals the 'fateful bargain'. The venturer must use trial and error methods to develop the construct system that will guide him/her to the behaviors that will not invalidate segments of the construct systems of members of the entrenched population. Will dinner guests appreciate opening the meal with slices of pungent processed meats? How much body contact will be allowed during the leave-taking as the guests depart? Should the host proudly proclaim that the salad greens were grown organically in his back yard garden? More generally, shall the venturer serve the salad before the main course because he believes that it is appropriate to do so, or will he succumb to that practice in order to ingratiate himself to his supervisor?

Even if the assimilation process were to prove extremely effective as a means of inducing immigrants to adopt construct systems that are totally compatible with those acquired my the majority of the members of the entrenched society, every society will face many other sources of invalidation.

Changes in the physical world will produce one after another source of invalidation. People who construe themselves as healthy, active persons will fall to diseases that invalidate their self-defining psychollages. The earth will tremble, and the palaces will crumble; thus invalidating the self-defining psychollage of the nobleman who construes his self as the inhabitant of a luxury domicile. The customary rains will not fall during a summer season, and the peasant will experience invalidation of the psychollage of his self as a provider to his family.

Invalidations will be provided by other persons who invent novel psychollages through the use of metaphor, metonymy, synecdoche, and irony. A 'madman' will vociferously insist that his self-guiding narratives are based on correctly defining his self as the victim of a vast conspiracy aimed at turning all virile American men into gays. Political 'radicals' will regularly appear to claim that one must use novel psychollages in order to construe 'correctly' the development of beneficent social structures.

The observation in the last sentence is intended to direct attention to adopting a constructivist perspective to practices for dealing with invalidation. The major step requires considering what is meant by 'correct construing' and moving toward agreement with Kerby's claim that:

... The truth of our narratives does not reside in their correspondence to the prior meaning of prenarrative experience; rather, the narrative is the meaning of the prenarrative experience. *The adequacy of the narrative cannot, therefore, be measured against the meaning of prenarrative experience but properly speaking, only against alternative interpretations of that experience.* (Kerby, 1991, p. 84)

Many problems will remain, of course, when such constructivist epistemology becomes 'common sense'. There will always remain the problems of how a society shall respond to persons who would subvert or resist the process of reaching necessary agreement on how to construe an event and then refuse to use the psychollages that have been endorsed by the social group.

Additionally, even a society that assiduously uses a constructivist epistemology will encounter conditions that can arise from accumulation of power in its many manifestations – financial, physical, intellectual, and so forth. By displays of power which serve to relieve him/her from experiencing the arousal associated with invalidation of his/her construct system, the holder of power can readily divert focus from the relevant issues in the process of achieving co-construction in order to shift focus to the tangential issues – issues other than the necessity of exploring the necessity of maintaining or forgoing the use of favored construction systems.

References

Addams, J. (1912). *Twenty years at Hull House with autobiographical notes.* New York: The Macmillan Company.

Banfield, E. C. (1958). *The moral basis of a backward society.* New York: Free Press.

Christopher, R. C. (1987). *Crashing the Gates: The de-WASPing of America's elite.* New York: Simon and Schuster.

Cubberly, E. *Changing conceptions of education.* Boston: Houghton Mifflin, 1909.

D'Acierno, P. (1999). Cinema paradiso: The Italian American presence in American cinema. In P. D'Acierno (Ed.) *The Italian American heritage: A companion to literature and arts* (pp. 563-690). New York: Garland Publishing, Inc.

Davenport, C. B. (1911). *Heredity in relation to eugenics.* New York; Henry Holt.

Dickie, J. (1999). *Darkest Italy: The nation and stereotypes of the mezzogiorno, 1860-1900.* New York: St. Martin's Press.

Fransella, F. (Ed.). (2003). *International handbook of personal construct psychology.* London: John Wiley & Sons.

Gans, H. J. (1982). *The urban villagers: Groups and class in the life of Italian-Americans.* New York: Free Press.

Gibson, M. (2002). *Born to crime : Cesare Lombroso and the origins of biological criminology.* Westport, Ct., Praeger.

Goddard, H.H. (1912). *The Kallikak Family: A study in the heredity of feeblemindedness.* New York: Macmillan Company.

Italic Studies Institute (2002) *Research project: Italian culture on film* (1928-2002). http://italic.org/imageb1.htm

Kelly, G. A. (1991/1955). *The psychology of personal constructs*. New York: Routledge. (Original work published 1955).

Kerby, A. P. (1991). *Narrative and the self*. Bloomington, IN: Indiana University Press.

Kevles, D. J. (1985). *In the name of eugenics*. Berkeley: University of California Press.

Lissak, R. S. (1989). *Pluralism & progressives: Hull house and the new immigrants. 1890-1919*. Chicago: University of Chicago Press.

Mancuso, J. C. (1996). Constructionism, personal construct psychology, and narrative psychology. *Theory and Psychology, 6*, 47-70.

Mancuso, J. C. (2000). Key signifiers of a constructivist psychological theory. http://www.capital.net/~mancusoj/pcpsigfr.html .

Mancuso, J. C., Ceely, S. G. (1980) The self as memory processing. *Cognitive Therapy and Research, 4*, 1-25.

Mancuso, J. C., Sarbin, T. R. (1983). The self-narrative in the enactment of roles. In T. R. Sarbin, K. Scheibe (Eds.), *Studies in social identity* (pp. 233-253). New York: Praeger Press.

Mancuso, J. C., Sarbin, T. R. (1998). The narrative construction of emotional life: Developmental aspects. In Mascolo, M. F. and Griffin, S. (Eds.), *What develops in emotional development?* (pp. 297-316). New York: Plenum.

Mancuso, J. C., Rossellini, R. (2001). Italian-American culture meets the dominant culture of the northwest USA. http://www.capital.net/~mancusoj/suzzpell.html

Mangione, J., Morreale, B. (1992). *La storia: Five centuries of the Italian American experience*. New York: Harper Collins.

Mascolo, M. F., Mancuso, J. C. (1990). The functioning of epigenetically evolved emotion systems. *International Journal of Personal Construct Psychology, 3*, 205-220.

Orsi, R. A. (1985). *The Madonna on of 115th Street*. New Haven: Yale University Press.

Pellegrini, A. (1984). *The unprejudiced palate*. San Francisco: North Point Press (Originally published in 1948, by McMillan).

Pellegrini, A. (1986). *America dream: An immigrant's quest*. San Francisco: North Point Press.

Salins, P. D. (1997). *Assimilation, American style*. New York: Basic Books.

Schneider, J. (Ed.) (1998). *Italy's "southern question:" Orientalism in one country*. New York: Oxford.

After 40 years of peace - war in the heart of Europe[39]

Du_an Stojnov

A couple of years ago, at the dawn of the conflict in former Yugoslavia, a friend of mine asked me "in what important way are the Serbs different from the Croats?" For some reason, we were interrupted and I never managed to answer her properly. However, the question stayed with me all these years and provoked numerous reflections and elaboration.

Although the problem of political conflict is not exclusively psychological in nature, it inevitably has comprehensive psychological implications, as Kelly (1962) has shown in 'Europe's matrix of decision'[40]. Highlighting the issue seems to represent the process of finding a "...basis for slicing off chunks of time and reality and holding them up for inspection one at a time", rather than being "...left swimming in a shoreless stream, where there are no beginnings and no endings to anything" (Kelly, 1955; p. 120). Therefore, this article is a step towards proposing relevant axes of meaning through which the conflict in former Yugoslavia should be considered. It is also my personal attempt to find an 'antidote' to the prevailing political reductionism of the media which have created a rather preemptive construction of '*Serbia contra mundum*'.

Yugoslav matrix of dimensions

The first dimension to be considered is *ethnical*. Within those parts of former Yugoslavia that are in conflict, the ethnic composition is the following: there are three ethnic groups, Croats, Serbs and Muslims, as well as a couple of ethnic minorities, of which the biggest are the Albanians and Hungarians. All of the major ethnic groups are of Slav origin, and they came to the Balkan peninsula during the sixth and seventh centuries, A.D. After the rise and expansion of the Ottoman Empire, a significant number of the originally Slav population, namely the Croats and Serbs, were converted to Islam. The Yugoslav Muslims were not recognised as an ethnic group until 1974, when they were recognised as a 'Muslim' nation.

---

[39] Reprinted from Scheer, J. W., Catina, A. (Eds.) (1996): *Empirical constructivism in Europe – The personal construct approach.* Giessen: Psychosozial-Verlag (43-51).
[40] Reprinted in this volume, p. 12-44 *(Ed.)*

Very close to the ethnic, but not fully parallel with it, is the *religious* dimension. With a somewhat simplified view of the problem, one can consider the war in Yugoslavia as an epiphenomenon of the core conflict between the Western and Eastern Roman Empires, that resulted in a religious dualism (Catholic vs. Orthodox), continuing as a dualism in culture, politics, ideology, that finally led to disintegration. After the split of the Roman Empire into an Eastern and Western half, and the subsequent schism in the Roman Church, the Eastern parts of Yugoslavia, i.e. Serbia, Montenegro and Macedonia, followed Orthodox Christianity, while the Western parts developed along the lines of the Catholic tradition. Turkish dominance over the Balkan peninsula led some Christians to convert to Islam in order to escape the atrocities dealt out by the local Turkish authorities. During the five hundred years of Turkish occupation, Islam was augmented and it survived even after the fall of the Ottoman empire and the retreat of the Turks from the occupied provinces.

The Hegelian view that a nation does not make history unless it has a state goes perhaps some way towards explaining the political processes in Yugoslavia. Therefore, the next dimension is labelled *statism,* which stands for the tendencies of different ethnic groups to have independent and free countries. The first Slavic medieval states were Croatia, with its own dynasty, and the two Serbian states of Serbia and Bosnia, with their own dynasties of Serbian origin. The relationship of statism to ethnicity and religion is the same as between religion and ethnicity: they are not on a one to one basis. Countries come and go, although in time cycles that usually last longer than individual human lives. This has involved a loss of independence for Croatia, which was conquered by the beginning of the twelfth century, and Serbia and Bosnia who lost their independence in the middle of the fourteenth century. Nevertheless, after a long time, they all came to life. Serbia and Montenegro had their own kingdoms in the nineteenth century, and after the First World War the common Kingdom of Serbs, Croats and Slovenes - later transformed into Yugoslavia was proclaimed.

In order to explain all of the mentioned nations, religions and states without a diachronic approach would be static and uninformative. This leads us to a *historic* dimension. According to Kelly, "Man might be better understood if he were viewed in the perspectives of the centuries rather than in the flicker of the passing moments" (1955, p. 3). This calls for an inevitable historical analysis, sketched in rough details, in order to offer a wider perspective and the context in which the events occurred.

The former Croatian state lost its independence in the twelfth century, and since then has not been an independent state. Serbia's independence lasted for some three and a half centuries longer, before being conquered by the

Turks along with Bosnia. The next five hundred years saw Croatia and Slovenia conquered by Hungarians, and Serbia under Turkish reign.

One of the most frequent, pejorative descriptions of Yugoslavia is that it was an 'artificial' creation. Yet in 1918, when Yugoslavia came into existence, the new state seemed justified on several grounds. Its *original* name was the Kingdom of the Serbs, Croats and Slovenes, the multinational character of the country being thereby openly acknowledged. Yugoslavia was not simply carved out of the ruins of the Habsburg Empire. Its core were the kingdoms of Serbia and Montenegro, that had been fully independent since the 1878 Congress of Berlin (and were members of the victorious Allied coalition in the First World War). One of the former Habsburg possessions that joined the new state was Bosnia-Herzegovina, in which the Serbian population that lived alongside the Croat and Muslim Slavs formed the largest national group. In the Habsburg days Croatia was divided into three separate entities: Croatia proper, Slavonia and Dalmatia, the first two being nominally under the Hungarian crown. These lands also had large Serbian populations. Having been settled on this former military frontier of the Austrian Empire since the fifteenth century, preoccupation of these Serbs was fighting the Turks. In the Habsburg days they enjoyed a form of autonomy in Croatia. The Serbs were also the predominant nation in the Hungarian province of Vojvodina, another part of the collapsed Habsburg Empire that joined Yugoslavia, formerly by joining Kingdom of Serbia. At the time, the Habsburgs actually invited the Serbs to protect their borders from the Turks, so a considerable number of Serbian families were settled there. The Serbs and Croats had for centuries been divided by history and religion, but ethnically and linguistically, however, they are closely related. At the time of Yugoslavia's creation there was no history whatsoever of any Serbo-Croat wars. It was not until the First World War that regiments from Croatia in the army of the Habsburg Empire fought against Serbia. It is interesting to note that one of the Croatian participants in the war with Serbia was Josip Broz, later known as Tito. Finally, Slovenia, having been merely a province of Austria with never enough strength to form its own state was willing, in 1918, to join its fellow South Slavs in a new state.

The creation of Yugoslavia was a superordinated solution for different national interests. It completed the mission of successive Serbian governments to unite all Serbs in one state with the result of being part of a multinational country. Although some saw the new state as a 'Greater Serbia', the Serbs genuinely believed that they had liberated the Croats and Slovenes from the Habsburg yoke. On the other side, the Croats and Slovenes joined Yugoslavia with certain hard pragmatism in mind. Croatia and Slovenia were members of a defeated power. By uniting with Serbia in a new state they could reverse this situation, escape the destiny of defeated countries, and gain a favourable place at the post-war peace conference, something which Serbia, with its distinguished war record, was certain of. All in all, whatever the subsequent development, the creation of Yugoslavia made a great deal of sense in 1918. In terms of its national structure it was no more artificial than Czechoslovakia, Poland or Romania at the time. It was, in this sense, certainly less artificial than the Habsburg Empire.

The inter-war period in Yugoslavia was dominated by the Serbo-Croat dispute. The constitution of 1921 was of a unitary nature, concentrating administrative power in the capital, Belgrade. This was opposed by the Croats, who argued for a federate solution. The King, Alexander 1, dissolved the Parliament in 1929, suspended the constitution and assumed legislative powers. The name of the country was changed to Yugoslavia ('the land of South Slavs') in order to promote greater national unity. King Alexander I had become a Yugoslav nationalist, giving all opposition (Serbian and Croatian nationalists equally) a hard time. Extremism in Croatia began to flourish. The *Ustashe* ('uprising') movement aimed at complete independence for Croatia. This organisation was behind the 1934 assassination of King Alexander in Marseilles. The Croat question was finally addressed in 1939, when an agreement gave Croatia considerable autonomy.

The Serbo-Croat agreement came too late. In April 1941, Yugoslavia was invaded by Germany and its allies. The army fell apart, and the government fled into exile. The Croatian *Ustashe,* ideologically close to the Nazis, established an independent state of Croatia (although it was no more than a Nazi puppet state) which included Bosnia-Herzegovina. The stage was set, however, for the first Serbo-Croat war. The *Ustashe* carried out a policy of forced conversion of the Orthodox Serbs to Roman Catholicism. Worse still, perhaps as many as 700,000 Serbs were massacred in the concentration camp Jasenovac and elsewhere. The Serb insurgents retaliated, although on a much smaller scale. Their movement, the *Chetniks,* remained loyal to the government in exile. The Serbian 'Yugoslav Home Army' was conservative and royalist, and it was first to begin resistance to the Germans. Its tactics, though, were to fight them only sporadically in order to preserve strength and deal with the more menacing domestic enemies. *The Chetniks'* opponents included, in addition to *Ustashe,* the Yugoslav Communist Party, led by Josip Broz Tito. This party capitalised on the patriotism of many Yugoslavs, drawing additional support from those Serbs in Croatia who had not sided with *Chetniks,* and from disaffected Croats in *the Ustashe* state. By late 1943, the party and its resistance to the Germans succeeded in making Britain switch its previous support for the *Chetniks to* Tito's communists. The communists, however, were also fighting a vast and complex civil war. As many as a million Yugoslavs died at the hands of their countrymen in the Second World War. In late 1944, with the aid of Soviet arms, Tito forced the Germans out of Belgrade and became the victor in the Yugoslav tragedy. He founded the Federal People's Republic of Yugoslavia which later became the Socialist Federal Republic of Yugoslavia. A very similar situation to the one in the First World War took place. Although the independent state of Croatia was protected by the German Reich and had fought against the Allies, and in spite of its cruel efforts to have an ethnically 'clean' country, it again escaped the destiny of the defeated forces by becoming one of the Yugoslav republics.

The post-war communist phase either suppressed or mismanaged the national question. Tito established Yugoslavia as a federation of *six* republics: Serbia, Croatia, Slovenia, Macedonia, Bosnia-Herzegovina and Montenegro. The internal boarders were settled immediately after the war. The ethnic mix in Yugoslavia, however, was such that many communities, especially the widely dispersed Serbs, found themselves on the wrong side of the new borders. What made the borders acceptable was the fact that they did not have the character of state borders, but were merely indicators of the purely administrative competence of the different republics. Tito's wartime support among the Yugoslavs rested partly on the promise that the equality of nations would be respected. Once in power, he promoted the slogan of 'Brotherhood and Unity' and imposed a rigid centralised bureaucracy on the federation. The prevailing Marxist ideology dictated that nationalism be condemned as a reactionary force. However, leaders in some republics felt rather unhappy with this a-national and socialist Yugoslav unitarism. After 1974, Yugoslavia became a collection of rival states, when a new constitution increased the autonomy of the republics. This produced a cross between a federation and confederation in that the constituent republics and the two Serbian provinces of Vojvodina and Kosovo behaved like independent states in every respect, except in the areas of foreign policy and defence which remained centralised firmly in Tito's hands.

After Tito's death, centralism weakened, and the national problem rose again. The multi-party elections in 1990 gave a major boost to the confederate tendencies. Until June 1991, Yugoslavia retained, on the federal level, a defence force, a foreign policy and even the semblance of an economic policy, but the individual republics were pursuing parallel foreign and economic policies and, in the case of Croatia, formed their own armed forces. Slovenia raised the question of secession. Transition was inevitable. Unfortunately, it was followed by disintegration which was based on the republic borders, and again it left many on the wrong side of these borders. The outbreak of war in mid-1991 opened up tantalising prospects for the republics. They could aim for outright independence, seek territorial revision, and try at least to satisfy whatever aspirations they had in the general chaos that now characterised Yugoslavia.

Out of the fear that remaining in Yugoslavia would lead to a Serbian dominance of the Croats, the Croatian leadership unearthed the symbols from *the Ustashe era* - and this was seen as a threat of atrocities by the Serbs against them. The situation exploded first in the multiethnic regions of Croatia and Bosnia. After just one act by the United Nations (recognition of administrative borders as international state borders), Croatian and Bosnia Serbs lost their country and found themselves in a foreign, and very hostile environment. Pre-empting the Croats as murderers, they did not want to wait for another Jasenovac. They were armed and ready this time. The only channel for communication left was the language of arms. The river of blood flowed once more.

Different history calls for a specific *political philosophy*. The political philosophy of medieval Serbia was expansionist, tending to succeed over Byzantium and give a new breath to the Eastern Roman Empire.

Thoroughly invalidated by the Ottomans, the goal of political philosophy for the Serbs in the last two centuries diminished to a principle of integrity and wholeness, which meant uniting the Serbian Diaspora in one country. The political philosophy of Croatia after 1102 was founded on a single aim: the attainment of independence from the Austrian and Hungarian invaders, with the hope of reviving the Croatian state.

But there are a thousand ways to skin a cat. The same aim in political philosophy can be achieved by different *ideologies*. Monarchy, democracy, parlamentarism, totalitarism, liberalism, socialism, nationalism, internationalism, communism and a myriad of other 'isms' were present in the history of Yugoslavia and the different nations comprising it. They were also the cause of numerous conflicts even before disintegration in 1992.

The dimension of *superstatism* refers to the part which other international factors, such as neighbouring countries, big political forces and alternative centres of power (e.g. The Vatican, etc.) have in the formation of certain states, making it anything but an internal affair. Unfortunately, the formation of the independent countries of South Slavs was always governed by the pragmatic interests of diplomacy of the big forces. The outcome of the Serbian uprising against the Turks was sealed in the British Parliament. Just one debate between Disraeli and Gladstone led to the death of thousands of rebels (Maurois, 1953). The destiny of the integration of South Slavs and the creation of Yugoslavia was decided at the congresses and conferences in Berlin in 1978, Versailles in 1919 and Yalta in 1943; never within its own territory or by its own rulers. The same goes for its disintegration. The Yugoslav crisis, and specially its descent into violence, came to be seen as the great anomaly of post-Cold War Europe. The international community was certainly not indifferent towards the conflict in Yugoslavia, for it had far-reaching implications. The danger existed that the fighting could assume wider regional proportions by involving some of its neighbours. Some were concerned about the fate of their minorities, while others recalled their historic interests and ambitions in Yugoslavia.

Different ethnic groups in different countries with different religions result in different *cultures,* which represent the eighth dimension. Although speaking the same language, the Croats, and Serbs use different alphabets: Latin by the former and Cyrillic by the latter. They also have different myths, different taboos and, by and large, different folk customs, which have resulted in the formation and development of notably different social and cultural identities.

Last but not least is the ninth, *economic* dimension. During the period after the Second World War, there was an obvious discrepancy between the more developed economies of the western Yugoslav republics of Slovenia and Croatia and the relatively undeveloped central and eastern regions in Bosnia, Serbia, Montenegro and Macedonia. This was partly due to Tito's policy in removing Serbian industry from Serbia after the break with Stalin in 1948, and placing it in the western parts of the country. It was not surprising that the economically more developed republics advocated a less federate and less unitaristic leadership, favouring the view that their economical stability was dragged down by the rest of the country. This claim reached its climax in the secessionist policy of Croatia and Slovenia. On the other side, the eastern and southern republics accused Croatia and Slovenia of industrial colonialisation and exploitation.

Different hypotheses, different anticipations

The overview of dimensions presented above highlights the context in which, over a couple of centuries, different hypothesis were formed and subsequently tested. The Croats see the Serbs as an obstacle to their own national state, the first after almost a thousand years. The Croatian and Bosnian Serbs see nothing but atrocities against them from now on if they stay in „foreign" countries. The Serbs in Serbia see the new independent states of Croatia and Bosnia, acknowledged by United Nations, as a cutting off and abandonment of almost a third of their population outside its borders.

The major problem here is that every anticipated strategy mentioned above which could satisfy one side, necessarily leads to invalidation of a solution constructed by another. It is very difficult to imagine a superordinated position which can be broad enough to satisfy both sides. The validation of the core national interests (constructs) of one side would make the other side aware of imminent comprehensive change in its own core structure.

This inevitably leads to the question of transition. It seems that some of the dimensions of transition can equally be applied to both societies and persons. But countries in transition also involve people in transition. Unfortunately, the problem is in that the time cycles for societies and humans are on different scales. What could be a short period of transition for a country or a nation, can last as long as a person's whole life, a life of cumulated threat for the majority of people living in the parts of the former Yugoslavia. And when threatened, people usually do not construe propositionally or stay open to revision. They need at least some control over the elements of their construing. Preemption seems to be the only choice left, with hostility waiting around the corner. This leads towards construing the 'enemy' as hostile, threatening and nothing but dangerous. And from such danger we must defend ourselves. Fighting against the other side seems to be the only reasonable choice. Choosing war seems to be a rational choice, as rational as choosing between going to the cinema or going to the theatre: For the Serbs, the only alternative to going to war is being slaughtered by the institutions of the newly formed Croatian government, as they were in 1941. For the Croats, the alternative to fighting and exterminating the Serbs from 'their' country means losing the territory inhabited by the Serbs, thus being fragmented, divided and dominated by the Serbs in Yugoslavia. Bosnia, which is inhabited by Serbs, Croats and Muslims, has three groups which seem to have nothing in common. The Croats want to unite with Croatia, the Serbs with Serbia and the Muslims want to have an Islamic state of their own. But the major point is that all sides are threatened by each other, and that one's validation of the core construing seems to be the core invalidation of the other.

A hint towards solution

A good divorce seems to be a much better solution than a bad marriage. The only problem is how to make the split with all the conflicting claims. Unfortunately, it seems that the *ethical* dimension does not find its place in the range of convenience of political construing. It is being reduced to the utopian dream of the small and helpless, envying the big and powerful on whom they depend for so many important core issues - such as independence, autonomy, integrity and freedom.

It may appear hostile, but I still believe that the construct of good vs. evil is not void of meaning. If all proposed axes of meaning could be replaced by a single dimension, my proposal would be *ethical.* If there is any possible solution for the conflict in Yugoslavia, it can be reached only through a formal, universal ethical principle. This calls for justice and social equality. In PCP terms, it implies prepositional construing and the role relationship. It could be construed as the outcome of an agreement of all the sides involved in conflict, based on mutual understanding and dialogue. It seems that only this alternative has not been tested to date, and that all other solutions have failed so far. Without this approach, the problem will return in less than fifty years in the form of another drastic experimentation involving new atrocities and destruction. It was not solved properly in 1919, and it returned in 1941. It was mistreated in 1943, and it burst out again in 1991. It seems to be a theme which permeates Yugoslav history from its very beginning. A theme obviously representing some core issues which have not been dealt with successfully.

What practical conclusions can be drawn from all of this? Does a constructivist approach offer any solution to a problem which is remote from the realm of clinical psychology and personality, such as the war in the heart of Europe? Watzlawick's explanation of the implications which the acceptance of reality as someone's construction has, speaks for itself:

> *First of all, ...such a person would be tolerant. If we come to see the world as our own invention, we must apply this insight to the world of our fellow creatures. If we know that we do not or cannot know the truth, that our view of the world is only more or less fitting, we will find it difficult to ascribe madness or badness to the world views of others. Second, such a person would feel responsible, in a very deep ethical sense, not only for conscious decisions and actions, ...but for the reality created* (Watzlawick, 1984; p. 326-327).

I wonder if this has any meaning for generals and politicians?

P.S. (2003): *As a result of its very turbulent recent history, Yugoslavia has changed its name to 'Serbia and Montenegro'.*

References

Kelly, G. A. (1955). *The Psychology of Personal Constructs*, New York: Norton.
Kelly, G. A. (1962). Europe's Matrix of Decision. In: Jones, M. R. (ed.): *Nebraska Symposium on Motivation.* pp. 83-123. Lincoln: Nebraska University *Press. (reprinted in this volume)*
Maurois, A. (1953): *Dizraeli*, Beograd: Prosveta.
Watzlawick, P. (1984): Epilogue. In: Watzlawick, P. (ed.): *The invented reality*. New York: Norton.

Persons in contexts: personal-human values and foreign cultures[41]

Bill Warren

A Vignette

On 26 July, 1993 I received a telephone call from Jörn Scheer and Ana Catina, telephoning from Alice Springs, central Australia, wishing me 'Happy Birthday'. It was a few days after the 10th International Congress on Personal Construct Psychology in Townsville where, I assume, I had mentioned a forthcoming 'birthday'. Jörn and Ana had decided to see some of the 'red centre' and found themselves in Alice Springs as part of their wish to see Uluru (Ayers Rock). Surprise and delight, exchange of pleasantries about aging and the weather gave way to a serious question Jörn raises. This is whether he and Ana should abide by a notice on the wall of a pub indicating that people/tourists should not buy alcohol for black/aboriginal/indigenous people. Wise, 'local' knowledge is asked for and I say as follows. If the notice was displayed by white/non-indigenous people, then ignore it; if it was displayed by indigenous people themselves, for example by elders or other leaders, then obey it. Does that help? "Well. Yes. But only, if we know by whom the notice was put up in the first place!?"

This real life experience says a good deal about the manner in which three friends seek a construction of a situation that will satisfy a number of concerns that each might have, concerns to make the best sense of a circumstance or situation, to reach a satisfactory meaning, a shared meaning. In this Chapter, I discuss my own construction of the situation, and my construction of their constructions.

For me, the experience recounted in the vignette raises numerous issues, but I here consider several basic ones. There are three basic issues that come to my mind, though some tangential others may also appear: an understanding of how individual sovereignty, rights and freedoms might be construed; the personal construction of the social-cultural context in which Australians find themselves in relation to this land's indigenous peoples; and, finally, my construction of, and of the constructions of, others. The first two are taken-up in Section I, the third in Section II.

---

[41] This paper was originally published in German as: Warren, B. (2001). Menschen im Kontext: persönlich-menschliche Werte und fremde Kulturen. in: J. Scheer (Ed.) (2001). *Identität in der Gesellschaft*. Giessen: Psychosozial-Verlag. (38-50). *(Ed.)*

I

The notion that any one person or group might legitimately impose their will on another is a most curious one and one which has attracted some, but little, attention. Social philosophers at least since Aristotle have written much on systems of government and related issues of law, civil and civic rights, disobedience, justice and so forth, but only a few have taken the question back to a more radical level. That is, few have examined the fundamental basis of sub and super-ordination or argued and concluded that government is inherently invalid, a relationship of sub- and superordination never justified, the *de jure* state never legitimate. This last position is acknowledged as at least arguable and the perspective known as Anarchism, which argues it, recognised by no less an authority than the *Encyclopaedia Britannica*. An entry on Anarchism was included in its 1905, Eleventh edition, a dispassionate entry written by the Russian anarchist Peter Kropotkin (1842-19210).

More generally, the question of whether the State is a legitimate entity entitled to obedience has seen periods in which such an idea was debated and challenged, and periods like the present where it appears to be of less general interest. In the period when it was debated and challenged, Wolff (1970) argued that anarchism was the only coherent position because there was no philosophical justification for the *de jure* legitimacy of the State. Thus, "philosophical anarchism would appear to be the only reasonable political belief of an enlightened" person (p. 19).

One of the most enthusiastic and theoretically thorough expounders of this view was Peter Kropotkin (1842-1921) who reviewed the social theory that is Anarchism, a review constituting the entry in the *Encyclopaedia Britannica* into the 1960s, and concluded that Anarchism was a principle of life itself:

> *Anarchism ... [is] the name given to a principle or theory of life and conduct under which society is conceived without government. ... In a society developed on these lines, the voluntary associations which already now begin to cover all the fields of human activity would take a still greater extension so as to substitute themselves for the State in all its functions. They would represent an interwoven network, composed of an infinite variety of groups and federations of all sizes and degrees, local, regional, national and international - temporary and more or less permanent - for all possible purposes: production, consumption and exchange, communications, sanitary arrangements, education, mutual protection, defence of the territory, and so on. (Anarchism; Baldwin, 1927/1970, p.284).*

The same period that saw Wolff's (1970) return to the fundamental question saw others also resurrecting Kropotkin's thought. Capouya and Tompkins (1976) insisted on the perennial value of Kropotkin's ideas, and Goodman

(1968), who is better known to us for his work in Gestalt Therapy (Perls, Hefferline, and Goodman, 1951), highlighted the value of Kropotkin's ideas for the 'heady' days of the 1960s. In each case what was stressed was an ideal of people working together to secure the fundamentals of life, and, then, developing understandings of the human predicament in dialogue freed from power-seeking and 'ready-made' views of things, which views were imposed on them.

Kropotkin's anarchism grew from his experience of the kindness of ordinary people, on the one hand, and of the corruption and the vagaries of personality in holders of High Office on the other. He saw the last as he trained at the Court of the tsars Alexander I and II, and went on to became a soldier in a Cossack regiment serving in Siberia, and, amongst other things, suffered imprisonment at different points in a career that also saw him write of prison reform as an administrator, thus seeing prisons from 'both sides'. He established himself as a distinguished scholar in the field of Geography, mapping the territory between Siberia and China, and was invited to join the Royal Society in the United Kingdom; an honour he turned down because of the connotations of the term 'royal'. Kropotkin sought to show that there was an important capacity operating in life, a capacity to help one another, to co-operate, to engage in *mutual support*. He argued that this operated in human history just as powerfully and, indeed, was more conducive to survival than was competitiveness and aggression. However, it served certain interests better to emphasise competitiveness and aggression in order to justify a strong centralised state so as to ensure so called 'law and order'.

These are high sounding ideas, abstract and theoretical, and in revisiting his earlier sympathetic survey (Woodcock, 1963), Woodcock (1986) recognises the current world reality where advanced technology dominates and complex financial and other dimensions interact, thereby making Anarchist ideas impractical. Nonetheless, he reaffirms the value of the outlook taken by the anarchists, an ideal that challenges a too ready acceptance of any 'common wisdom' about a complex reality that is to be allowed to rationalise the domination of the individual, or the domination of one group by another.

Whatever the viability of these ideas about personal sovereignty and resistance, however, it might by now being asked: what have they to do with the present discussion? The answer is that they locate my own construction of a circumstance or situation in which some prohibition or restriction is being placed on another person, or a position of superordinancy claimed and enforced. To understand my construction of the circumstance Jörn and Ana had described and for which they sought guidance, one must see how any such guidance I might offer grows out of a broader construct system that is nurtured by a long history of interest in those ideas that go to fundamental questions about our social life and relationships.

178

In addition, however, that understanding of my understanding must also have regard to another dimension of my construing drawn from the type of information that I amassed during my formative years, and beyond. These last concern a 'real world' context in which Aboriginal people live their lives; the situation in which both so called Aboriginal and non-Aboriginal people find themselves in Australia.

The real world situation of Aboriginal Australians is complex and fraught with practical, ideological and political questions in addition to more scholarly ones of no less practical import. This last is reflected, for example, in a debate over whether white Europeans 'invaded' or 'settled' this continent. The history taught to me was that the country had been settled, that the indigenous people were one of the most primitives on the planet, living in 'humpies', with poor personal hygiene, with no significant cultural or religious traditions. We (white Anglo-Saxon Europeans) had brought them all the benefits of European civilisation and they should be grateful to be inducted into the Christian way of life as they had but the most primitive account of the origins of life and the creation of humankind. I was taught that these people offered little resistance to white settlement, and if they did it was clearly in breach of the system of law brought to this country and they were justly punished for such resistance.

The fact that there were warriors who did strenuously resist the European invasion of their country was not taught. The fact that Europeans murdered hundreds of Aboriginal people, including women and children, was overlooked. That some European men took woman as 'comfort women' and disposed of them as 'objects' was also overlooked. The killing of other people's cattle or sheep on which the life and livelihood of the settler-invaders relied, was highlighted, but less so the perspective of a people who had different outlook on ownership. Yet, for balance, we must also acknowledge that with the questionable benefits of conversion to one or other Christian dogma - either Catholic or Protestant as these two perspectives represented essentially by Catholic Irish convicts and Protestant English overseers vied for dominance in the colony - came a facility with reading and writing that is hard to judge not to be a good.

There is even a further dimension to these matters already subsumed in my observations about 'Aboriginal people' or 'indigenous people' as if they were a homogeneous group. As Heitmeyer (1998), for example, reminds us there are many different groups who lived in different localities and had different cultures: "Before 1770 the Australian continent comprised over 500 hundred different peoples, each with their own language and stories" (p. 197). Further, there is a history of an obsession with 'defining' an indigenous person, represented in earlier times by efforts of administrators to establish a 'blood content'; efforts as impossible as they were ill-conceived. These efforts gave way to a more pragmatic and sensible approach required by programs aimed at ameliorating social inequities, thus requiring identification of those who were eligible for assistance. Factors in this identification were that a person was a descendant of an indigenous person, identified him or her self as such, and was accepted as such by the community in which he or she lived.

It is easy for a - for this - city dweller to range across these matters, living comfortably in a community where there are few people of Aboriginal descent and few social problems arising for them by my presence here. Thus is there a gulf between the city and 'the bush' in regard to a range of issues pertaining to relations between indigenous people in Australia. It is this gulf that is capitalised on by some politicians, and this is manifested in two particular developments. The one is the emergence of a new Australian political Party, One Nation, with origins in 'the bush', a Party which alleges, and with little regard to history, that government treatment of indigenous Australians as unfair to other Australians in that it gives indigenous people advantages not enjoyed by other Australians. The second manifestation of this city-country divide is the refusal of the current, conservative Prime Minister of Australia to say 'sorry', specifically to those indigenous people, and to their families, who were taken from their families as children in a perhaps well-meaning but culturally insensitive way.

The experience in many country towns is of drunkenness, violence, and crime; drunkenness generated by alcohol purchased at non-Aboriginal owned outlets. How frustrated can a community become with this reality, and perhaps how shortsighted is reflected in 'mandatory sentencing' which takes away the authority of a Magistrate or Judge to match a punishment to a crime after taking all of the personal and social circumstances of the accused or convicted person into account. Mandatory sentencing means prison, and prisons expose Aboriginal people, especially males, to significant risk of death, even when their crimes are modest ones. The Australian Royal Commission into Aboriginal Deaths in Custody (RCIADIC) noted that Aboriginal people in custody do not die at a higher rate than non-Aboriginal people, but that Aboriginal people are overwhelmingly over-represented in custodial contexts (Cunneen, 1997, p. 3). Moreover, the primary reason for Aboriginal people finding themselves in prisons or like places goes to matters of general disadvantage and inequality expressed in such things as poor health and housing, limited educational opportunity, and unemployment.

There is, then a reality of social problems, and centred in these is alcohol; or at least excessive use of alcohol and related psychological and social problems. The 'why' of this may be biological, or it may be an outcome of converting, through circumstance or intention, a hunter-gatherer into a fringe dweller in his or her own country. Whatever the reasons, alcohol has become a major problem, particularly in country Australia. But, whether a prohibition is justifiable, especially one imposed by non-Aboriginal people, is an open question. Further, whether the problem can be taken from the broader and broadest context is another: "The Royal Commission saw disadvantage and inequality as linked directly to processes of disempowerment which had occurred through two hundred years of domination. In other words, contemporary Indigenous disadvantage was directly linked to the historical legacy of colonisation" (Cunneen, 1997, p. 4). Thus, there is now in place a raised consciousness concerning these matters, efforts to compensate disadvantage and to progress a process of reconciliation between Aboriginal and non-Aboriginal Australians.

Such is the social terrain of Jörn and Ana's question.

Yet, all of my observations are still a 'white' construal, and Aboriginal Australians see it differently. In a poem that is resonant with personal construct theory, West concludes:

> *Have you no shame when you tell, again*
> *'n again what you know I think; I'll tell*
> *you this my gubba man. I've changed*
> *your name to Fiction Inc. 'n while your*
> *mob, 'n some of mine, think your really*
> *grand; to me you only grate.*

(Japanangka Errol West, 1990's; cited in West, 1999)

Again, and closer to the psychology that draws Jörn, Ana and myself together is an account of some very relevant studies by Ross (1996), studies which bear directly on the present discussion. Ross (1996) provides an interesting account of the disparity between how the subject of housing is construed across cultures; forms of housing being inherently tied-in with culture. In her studies, Ross (1996) highlighted how non-Aboriginal people differed from Aboriginal people in that the former group tended to emphasise the built features of houses, against the latter group's emphasis on social aspects of houses. This last observation was related to her account of how Aboriginal people see any commonplace aspect of their lives, such as housing, as related to a longer-term view of their history and their relationship with non-Aboriginal people. Needless to say, their construing of the history of their contact with non-Aboriginal Australians differs from that of those non-Aboriginal people.

In our vignette we have a situation in which three people - Jörn, Ana and myself - attempt to share constructions of two groups of people: white residents of Alice Springs and local indigenous people. Perhaps, from the advice I had given there were in fact two different groups within the local indigenous group; that is, those who drank alcohol, and those 'elders' or leaders who tried to control its impact on their people and who displayed the Notice. We can even suggest further sub-groups arising from what we would call 'tribal alliances' of individuals and, further, another group who just did not drink alcohol at all. Ross (1996), a white Australian, indicated her own methodological dilemmas in her studies of Aboriginal Australians and their construing of housing, and this highlights the general problem of cross-cultural understandings. She also enlarges our frame of reference by noting different construing within an indigenous group, noting how an elderly male and a woman with children to care for see housing differently; indeed, as we all do. Ross' practical advice is to use a variety of methods to access the construing of members of a different culture. But the more telling outcome is that we *are* able to access and share the constructions of people of different cultures; while forms of life are different, the substance of the human struggle for existence and understanding remains the same.

My own perspective on the question raised by Jörn and Ana, as prompted by the experience recorded in the vignette, is clearer when seen as emerging from an egalitarian outlook on life drawn from an attraction to the type of social theory with which the present discussion was opened. The compatibility of this with personal construct psychology is one of the attractions for me of this psychology and I have suggested elsewhere (Warren, 1996) that a psycho-social dimension grounded in a concept of democratic or egalitarian mentality is both necessary to and latent within personal construct psychology. Further, I have had my early constructions of Aboriginal life and behaviour significantly invalidated as I grew, travelled, developed, listened and learned. And my understandings of these last matters are very much 'alive' in present day Australia where the historical trials and the current plight, as well as the contribution and the promise of indigenous culture, are very much under discussion and, sometimes, elaboration.

II

I must construe Jörn's and Ana's constructions in terms of expanding and elaborating my own construct system in which they occupy a place. I have more than a passing acquaintance with Jörn, one that goes a little way beyond a merely collegial relationship. It embraces a visit to my home and an introduction to my non-academic friends and to our local community life. I know Ana principally through personal construct psychology conferences, as well as the social dimensions thereof, and from Email conversations. I bring to my construing concerning Jörn a modest knowledge of German culture, what I would assert was a good knowledge of German Philosophy, and, of course, the stereotypes that infect us all. I bring a very restricted knowledge of Romania, coupled with some narrow insights through the eyes of an angry, depressed client who had fled that country, leaving his family, to make a life in Australia.

With these understandings - or lack of them - in place when the question to which the vignette refers was raised, I would have construed Jörn and Ana's request for advice as emerging from a personal-social-cultural context. The European social-cultural context from whence Jörn and Ana came I construe as well-informed (including informed about Australia), sophisticated, and significantly 'politicised'. My constructions of the personal dimension would emphasise high principles, morality, admirable efforts to understand and properly respond to the context in which they found themselves, to avoid offence to either indigenous or non-indigenous people and, obviously, a questioning outlook.

A little exercise helps test these ideas and locates my constructions as they are now. This takes the form of my completion of a Repertory Grid that I sometimes use with clients, including on this occasion Jörn and Ana as Elements. The other supplied Elements are familiar role titles and relationships: father, mother, best friend, sibling, spouse, most moral person, happiest person, and the like. Constructs are supplied and are drawn from a pool of those common to interpersonal relationships; such constructs as *calm-anxious*, *responsible-irresponsible*, *warm-cold*, *confident-anxious*, *democratic-authoritarian*. The implications of *supplying* constructs and elements are not lost on me, but at least these are 'my' constructs and elements.

The data was analysed using Slater's (1976) program INGRID. Not surprisingly, given the particular set of elements used, neither Jörn nor Ana figured as important elements, accounting for only a small percentage of the variance in the Principal Components Analysis in each case. The element 'Jörn' loaded on Component Two of the analysis (18%) which was defined in terms of constructs *confident, not gullible, not frightened,* and *acumen.* The element 'Ana' loaded on Component One of the analysis (48%) which was defined in terms of constructs *warm, don't hurt me, glad, understanding, easy going, flexible, shows affection,* and *unpretentious.* As an element, 'Jörn' was closest to 'Ana', and most distant from 'My Boss' (generally negatively construed). As an element, 'Ana' was closest to 'Most Successful Person', and most distant from 'My Worst Teacher'.

Thus might I have addressed the problem posed to me and outlined in the vignette with which we began, adding this personal dimension to the social-historical one that I have sketched. In the case of Jörn I imagine that at the time I imported into the question a construction involving a strong sense of responsibility, an intellectual rigour and confidence. In the case of Ana - rightly or wrongly - I have a sense of someone moving from one, perhaps politically and socially unstable country to another more stable country, and establishing herself without loss of self, wanting to 'do the right thing'. Indeed, my 'Most Successful Person' was a very good friend, recently deceased, who had come from humble beginnings and moved to a different social class, but had retained his old values, his 'success' lying in so doing. The closeness of Jörn and Ana in my construct system is likely not particularly significant given the relative artificiality of the exercise and the contrived purpose. Distancing Jörn from 'My Boss' likely is more significant in that my construal of German culture does likely derive from stereotypes of hierarchy, authority and stiffness, on the one hand, but personal experience of a more human and humorous individual than the stereotype embraces. Thus a 'boss' who might reasonably be seen in terms of a focus on hierarchy, but who does not present a human or humorous face, might be contrasted with Jörn. Ana's distance from a long-ago bad teacher is also mysterious here, but is likely understood in terms of that individual who was the 'Worst Teacher' coming from a privileged social class, unable to move away from an attitude of superiority in dealing with students who were not of that class; linked, again, to success having other than a material connotation.

My response to the question posed to me assumed two people who were socially and culturally sophisticated, attempting to act in a way that was consistent with their values and with what was in the best interests of the people at whom the Notice which had sparked their question was addressed. I knew them as reasonable people, people of principle and I saw them as people attempting to manifest personal-human values, which I construed us as sharing. I may have been, and may be, wrong. But I do not think so.

Conclusion

As there has been no argument, there ought to be no conclusion, but perhaps a final word is appropriate. Jörn, Ana, and myself are attracted to a psychology the focus of which is a person's, and Humankind's, understanding of his or her, or its, understanding. Jörn (1996[42]) himself sounded a warning about our complacency and potential hypocrisy as a wider group committed to personal construct psychology when the language of that very psychology and its Conferences is not the first language of all participants. But he also noted how his understanding of the understanding of others is given its best chance through the psychology of personal constructs.

Despite language and culture, Jörn, Ana, and myself have been able to communicate and to share understandings that assist the elaboration of each of our respective construings of the world. That we all perceived a problem in a pub in central Australia, that they sought an understanding of how to conduct

---

[42] Reprinted in this volume, p. 104-121 *(Ed.)*

themselves, and that I was then, and now, prompted to elaborate my own understandings, is not only a comment on ourselves, but also on the human predicament. That is, a being who cannot escape the construction of meaning and who must live with the fact that the particular meaning constructed is always imposed on that which may be „ultimately and forever meaningless", creating thereby a terrible irony (Rowe, 1978, p. 25). Whatever the immensity of the task ahead of us as individuals and as a species, just as constructive alternativism provides "a basis for insuring that people can indeed live together even though they construe the worlds they share differently" (Kalekin-Fishman & Walker, 1996, p. 384), so the experience construed in our vignette augers well for communication and for elaborating understandings.

Yet, at the time, I did not heed Jörn's then fresh advice. I did not respond in a relational language, talking of myself and the types of understandings of life, social relations and indigenous people that I held. Rather, I responded in a fashion that assumed a knowledge and a truth that I did not have. Perhaps I have here corrected that error, developing from a simple incident to expose a multifaceted context in which there are many different stories; certainly more stories than that of a city-dweller living 2000 kilometres from a town he had never visited.

In a tongue-in-cheek final, final word I close along the lines of the language I had used in my expression of thanks to Jörn for his presentation to the 10th International Congress, an observation which remains apt well beyond the specific situation of his contribution to that Congress. It is intended here as *relational*, even if it appears to be about power, control and exclusion. Such are the nuances of understanding in and across 'foreign' cultures that I am confident that those who read it will be able to gauge its meaning:

Well, G'day *and* good on ya, *Jörn. I wouldn't be* pulling your leg *if I said that you are a* bonza bloke, *who has made a* ripper *of a contribution to personal construct psychology. You're* allright, *a good* cobber *and a* fair-dinkum mate *to us all.*

References

Baldwin, R.N. (1970). *Kropotkin's revolutionary pamphlets*. New York: Dover Publications. (Original work published 1927. New York: Vanguard Press).

Capouya, E., Tompkins, K. (Eds.). (1976). *The essential Kropotkin*. London: The Macmillan Press.

Cunneen, C. (1997). *The Royal Commission into Aboriginal deaths in custody: An overview of its establishment, findings and outcomes*. Canberra: Monitoring and Reporting Section, ATSIC.

Goodman, P. (1968). Kropotkin at this moment. *Dissent*, 15, 519-522.

Heitmeyer, D. (1998). The Issue is not Black and White: Aboriginality and education. In J. Allan (Ed.). *Sociology of education*. Katoomba, NSW, Australia: Social Sciences Press.

Kropotkin, P. (1970). Anarchism. In R.N. Baldwin (Ed.), *Kropotkin's revolutionary pamphlets*, New York: Dover Publications Inc.

Perls, F., Hefferline, R. F., Goodman, P. (1951). *Gestalt Therapy*. New York: Dell Publishing Co., Inc.

Ross, H. (1996). Construing across cultures: Aboriginal people construe their housing and histories. In D. Kalekin-Fishman, B. Walker (Eds.). *The construction of group realities: culture, society, and personal construct theory*. Malabar, Florida: Krieger Publishing Company, 181-202.

Rowe, D. (1978). *The experience of depression*. London: John Wiley and Sons.

Scheer, J.W. (1996). 'Congress language', personal constructs, and constructive alternativism. In B.M. Walker, J. Costigan, L.L. Viney, B. Warren (Eds.). *Personal construct theory: a psychology for the future*. Melbourne: Australian Psychological Society. *(reprinted in this volume)*

Warren, W.G. (1996). The Egalitarian outlook as the underpinning of the theory of personal constructs. In D. Kalekin-Fishman, B. Walker (Eds.). *The construction of group realities: culture, society, and personal construct theory*. Malabar, Florida: Krieger Publishing Company, 103-119.

West, E. (1999). What should be the role of Aboriginal Studies at any of the three tiered systems of Australian education. In Craven, R. (Ed.). *Aboriginal studies: Educating for the future*. Collected papers of the 9th Annual ASA Conference, College of Indigenous Australian Peoples, Southern Cross University, Lismore, October, 1999. Sydney: Self-concept Enhancement and Learning Facilitation (SELF) Research Centre, University of Western Sydney, p.13-18.

Wolff, R.P. (1970). *In defence of anarchism*. New York: Harper.

Woodcock, G. (1962). *Anarchism*. Harmondsworth: Pelican.

Woodcock, G. (1986). *Anarchism*. Harmondsworth: Pelican (Second, revised edition).

APPENDIX

A short introduction to Personal Construct Psychology[43]

Jörn W. Scheer

Background

Readers not familiar with the Psychology of Personal Constructs might welcome a short introduction to the theoretical background of the papers compiled in this book. It can be short since there are several introductory books available in some of the major European languages. In English language, they are, among others, Bannister & Fransella (1986), Burr & Butt (1992), and Landfield & Epting (1987), in Italian Mancini & Semerari (1985), and in German Scheer & Catina (1993).

Even in the United States, Personal Construct Psychology cannot be considered a part of mainstream psychology. One of the reasons is that Kelly developed his theory in sharp contrast to the reigning schools of psychological thought of his time, behavioural theory and psychoanalysis. And to transport his new ideas, he chose to use a language and invented or re-defined terms not commonly used this way in academic psychology. Yet it is still a delightful experience to read especially the first three chapters of his main work (Kelly, 1955) where he elaborates the properties of a good theory and shows how Personal Construct Theory could serve as a major superordinate theory for many psychological phenomena.

Another point is concerned with the content of the theory. From the point of view of a 'nomothetic', would-be experimental behavioural psychology, Kelly's approach is provocatively subjectivist. Psychodynamically oriented psychologists may (erroneously) consider his theory being too cognitivist and lacking a thoroughly developmental perspective.

However, after the 'cognitive turn' of late in psychology, Kelly's theory seems to be more 'modern' than ever. On the other hand, with the relativistic ideas of constructivism, especially the 'radical' version having become more popular, Kelly's stance on empirical evidence (validation in his terms) has become increasingly attractive to researchers and practitioners who feel the need of empirical validation of their own concepts.

---

[43] An earlier version of this chapter appeared in Scheer & Catina (1996). *(Ed.)*

Personal Construct Theory

Anticipation

The limitation of space does not permit more than a very short overview of the basic concepts of the theory. Perhaps the most important idea is that of *anticipation*. Just as a scientist aims at a better control of reality by predicting events, every individual tries to predict the course of events in his/her life and to control their outcome. Every one of us has his/her explicit or implicit theories about the world around us (including the persons important to us), develops hypotheses and checks them against 'reality', in an almost experimental, in any case empirical way. Therefore *'man as scientist'* is the central metaphor of Kellyan theory. We anticipate events and experiences, we 'construe' our reality, and find our constructions eventually validated or invalidated and subsequently keep to them or modify them.

The 'fundamental postulate' of Personal Construct Theory therefore is:

> *A person's processes are psychologically channelized by the ways in which he anticipates events.*

In a number of 'corollaries', Kelly specifies these ideas, especially with respect to the properties of constructs and construct systems.

Constructs

Constructs are not just theoretical concepts as opposed to observable variables, like in standard psychology. Superficially, a construct is a verbal label, but this label represents a conceptual distinction that an individual makes. We are used to think in terms of contrasts (the *dichotomy* corollary): the concept of 'big' does not exist without an idea of 'small'.

It is important to note that constructs are not only names, or concepts, or attitudes, or opinions. Constructs have a function for the individual. In 'postmodern' talk, they have been called 'self-guiding narratives'. They serve as tools to replicate events in our imagination, and to make up our view of the world by continuous confirmation or disconfirmation, thus 'to construe reality' (the *construction* corollary). Constructs are organised in systems, often hierarchical in structure, there are superordinate constructs, core constructs, peripheral constructs, according to their importance to the individual's life (the *organisation* corollary). We have different construct systems for different areas and realms which may even be partially incompatible or at least contradictory when involved at the same time (the *fragmentation* corollary). Constructs in principle can be changed through experience (the *experience* corollary). A person decides for him/herself which alternative of a construct pertains to him/her, assigns him/herself to a construct pole, 'chooses' the construct pole, if he/she can expect an extension or definition of his/her construct systems. Doing this he/she 'construes him/herself' (the *choice* corollary). Constructs are significant characteristics of the individual (the *individuality* corollary), i. e. 'personal'. But the ways of construing of an individual are to some extent similar to those of another (the *commonality* corollary), and even if they are different - we have to be able to understand the other's constructions ('construe the other's constructions') (the *sociality* corollary) in order to be able to live in a society, to maintain interpersonal relationships. Every construct has a limited applicability (its range of convenience) and also an area where it fits best (the focus of convenience) (the *range* corollary). This also limits a construct's ability to change (the individual's capability of learning and re-orientation); the ability of a construct to include new events into its range of applicability may vary (the *modulation* corollary). Core constructs are central to the invidual's personality, they enable him/her to maintain his/her identity. They are superordinated to others, and have a wider range of convenience. If they are challenged and required to change, this is experienced as utterly stressful.

The focus of theoretical and practical interest of Personal Construct Psychology is the analysis of the construct systems which an individual uses to analyse, understand, structure, change his/her environment. One might say that in a Piagetian sense, the use of constructs encompasses assimilation as well as accommodation processes. And, as Kelly points out, in constructs emotions and cognitions are inseparably linked, and it does not make much sense to separate them and even assign them different kingdoms in the world of psychology.

Repertory Grid Technique

Kelly's theory would probably be less known and less influential, had he not invented an ingenious method of exploring constructs and construct systems: the Repertory Grid Technique. This is a kind of test that the 'subject' develops him/herself, guided by the psychologist. In a procedure described below the person first defines the area that the test is to be applied to (the 'elements'), then develops the items ('constructs'), then completes the grid that is made up by the two dimensions elements and constructs. In Kelly's original version (The Role Repertory Test), the famous 'significant others' constituted the elements. He had the subjects assign real persons to the 'role titles' supplied (such as father or favourite teacher). Then several selections of three elements each were compared *('please tell me, is there an important way in which two of these three* (you self, your father, and Auntie Nora) *are alike and thereby different from the third?'),* resulting in a list of bi-polar constructs. Finally the person had to decide which construct pole applied to every person (element) listed. A matrix (or grid) with 'ticks' and 'blanks' resulted that was considered a representation of the construct system pertaining to the set of elements involved. Nowadays, often a graded rating (e. g. on a 6-point scale) is used to assess the elements with respect to the constructs.

It can be seen that the information obtained is highly individual, therefore the technique has been termed 'idiographic'. However, the procedure is more or less standardised, which is an important feature of a procedure used in 'nomothetical' psychology. And, however personal the constructs are, certain properties of the construct *systems* can be distinguished and compared to those seen in other persons - irrespective of the *content* of the constructs.

Variations

The procedure described above is still the standard procedure of taking a 'repgrid' today. However a huge variety of topics have been explored in the research on construct systems - after all, we have construct systems for most every field of life (and death). In fact, in repgrid research elements as diverse as personal others, death situations, and British seaside resorts have been used. And the techniques of construct elicitation and of element assessments have been varied, too.

The main, almost revolutionary development however has been the application of mathematical analysis (principal component analysis and cluster analysis) to repgrid data using personal computers.

It may be seen from this that Repertory Grid Technique as a data collection method lends itself to a vast variety of applications. And it can also be used by researchers and practitioners who do not share the theoretical positions of Personal Construct Theory. Many of them are more interested in the interrelationship of the elements used - e. g. self-parent relationship, expressed in quasi-Euclidian distances, as representing 'object relations' in a psychoanalytical sense.

Other methods of exploring constructs

It has been argued that taking a repertory grid is comparable to a semistandardised interview, with the procedure being standardised, not the content. So it does not come as a surprise that other methods of exploring constructs have been developed. Among these are the 'laddering' and 'pyramiding' procedures which require the subject to successively explore the implications the constructs in question (and their poles) have for the person. Thus hierarchical relationships can be analysed better this way than through a repertory grid. A related technique is the ABC model which asks for the disadvantages and advantages of the opposite poles of a given construct for the person.

Controversies

Like other theories, Personal Construct Theory has a 'life', a kind of development in stages which has been described by R. Neimeyer (1985). The popularity of the Repertory Grid Technique has attracted persons with other theoretical observances. Some Personal Construct psychologists think that the time is right to reconsider theoretical orientations in view of the developments in other disciplines like cognitive psychology. The fact that the theory can be placed beside others with the idea of approximation, linkage, even amalgamating in mind, has been of concern to some of the leading theoreticians in Personal Construct Theory. On the other hand, 'orthodoxies in PCP' have already been identified and attacked. Kelly himself insisted on the limited 'range of convenience' of the theory and expected that at some time in the future it might become invalidated by the course of time. For the time being, however, PCP seems to be alive and well – as documented by the appearance of a new international handbook (Fransella, 2003) and a variety of Internet sites (see http://www.pcp-net.de).

References

Bannister, D., Fransella, F. (1986). *Inquiring Man* (3rd edition). London: Routledge.
Burr, V., Butt, T. (1992). Invitation to Personal Construct Psychology. London: Whurr.
Fransella, F. (Ed.). (2003). *International handbook of personal construct psychology*. London: Routledge.
Kelly, G.A. (1955). *The psychology of personal constructs*. Vols. 1 and 2. New York: Norton (2nd printing: 1991, London: Routledge).
Landfield, A., Epting, F. (1987). *Personal construct psychology: clinical and personality assessment*. New York: Human Sciences Press.
Mancini, F., Semerari, A. (1985). *La psicologia dei costrutti personali: saggi sulla teoria di G.A. Kelly*. Milano: Franco Angeli Libri.
Scheer, J.W., Catina, A. (Hrsg.) (1993). E*inführung in die Repertory Grid-Technik*, Bd. 1 und 2. Bern: Huber.
Scheer, J.W., Catina, A. (Eds.) (1996). *Empirical constructivism in Europe – the personal construct approach*. Giessen: Psychosozial Verlag.